The Anatomy of
Achievement Motivation

PERSONALITY AND PSYCHOPATHOLOGY:
A Series of Texts, Monographs, and Treatises

EDITED BY

Brendan A. Maher

The Anatomy of
Achievement Motivation

By Heinz Heckhausen

PSYCHOLOGISCHES INSTITUT
RUHR-UNIVERSITÄT
BOCHUM, GERMANY

Translated by KAY F. BUTLER, ROBERT C. BIRNEY,
and DAVID C. McCLELLAND

1967

ACADEMIC PRESS   New York and London

ACADEMIC PRESS INC.
111 Fifth Avenue, New York, New York 10003

United Kingdom Edition published by
ACADEMIC PRESS INC. (LONDON) LTD.
Berkeley Square House, London W.1

LIBRARY OF CONGRESS CATALOG CARD NUMBER: 66-29220

PRINTED IN THE UNITED STATES OF AMERICA

FOREWORD

German psychology has had important influences on American psychology at two different historical periods, first during its early beginnings when many Americans (from William James to Raymond Dodge) went to Germany to study and much later in the 1930's when prominent German psychologists like Köhler, Koffka, and Lewin came to this country to flee Nazism. What many American psychologists probably do not realize is that a whole generation of German psychologists has been developing since World War II—a generation greatly influenced by American psychology, and particularly by its methodological advances, from research design to factor analysis. I felt that Dr. Heckhausen's article should be translated, not just because it deals with achievement motivation, but because it should give American psychologists quite a new picture of the growth, importance, and sophistication of contemporary German psychology. Furthermore, Dr. Heckhausen's summary makes a contribution to knowledge that goes beyond anything in English on three counts: (1) It reviews not only the extensive experimental literature on achievement motivation in English, but also the considerable number of articles in German which, so far as I know, have not been covered in English summaries. (2) It integrates recent research and theory on achievement motivation with the earlier important tradition of research in Germany on the psychology of work, striving, success and failure, and level of aspiration. Oddly enough, these two approaches to very similar subject matter have been imperfectly combined in the United States; as he points out, this seems to have occurred in part because level of aspiration as a research technique seemed to get divorced from the problems in the psychology of achievement which it was supposed to illuminate. (3) It presents, in brief, a theoretical interpretation of what constitutes a motive which is rather different from the conceptions that have developed in the United States. American readers should be particularly interested in his picture of motivation as resulting from a cognitive "evaluative disposition" that, generally speaking, develops between 3½ and 4½ years of age.

Putting German into English that reads easily is extraordinarily difficult, as anyone who has tried it knows. The translators, with Dr. Heckhausen's full support, have often departed from the literal meaning of the German text in an effort to convey more clearly the author's intent, even though this has sometimes resulted in some extraordinary circumlocutions that still do not properly convey the original meaning. Take a very simple matter such as the translation of the word "Perspektive," which happens to have an English equivalent, "Perspective," which cannot be used in the same way. For some reason, "Perspective" has rather limited uses in English; we can speak of "perspective" in a drawing, or of having something in "perspective" without any trouble, but we are a little puzzled by the expression, "future time perspective" even though we recognize it as consisting of perfectly good English words. Does it mean (a) how far ahead one is looking in time, or (b) looking toward the future rather than the past, or (c) something else which is vaguer than either of these specific notions? In German, the term seems to include rather clearly the notion of observing in perspective a series of acts that take place in a certain order beginning at the present

moment and stretching out to some specific terminus in the
future. Perspective can have a "span" in German, but for
some reason it cannot in English (though attention can have a
"span" without any trouble!). In short, it involves a spatial
image (for which we use the word "perspective" in English
too) applied to time (which we do not use the word for ordi-
narily). Perhaps this will serve to illustrate how unhappy
translators must be with the results of their efforts. The task
has certainly made me a lot more sympathetic than I used to
be with the heroic translators who rendered Koffka into an
English that was still hardly readable. If we have erred, it is in
the other direction: We have tried, above all, to write in
readable English, even at the expense of literal correctness.

David C. McClelland

PREFACE

Personality psychology is, to a large extent, the study of individual differences in motivation. However, over recent years the personality psychologist has become increasingly concerned with identifying the determinants of specific motives, developing methods of measuring motive strength, and in recording the vicissitudes of motive-behavior relationships. In so doing, the psychologist has tended to turn from the earlier emphasis upon the integration of motives and from personality theorizing on the grand scale.

No finer example is to be found of the fruitfulness of the current approach than in the work on the achievement motive. Although Dr. Heckhausen rightly points out that interest in achievement motivation dates back to 1910, he makes it clear that until an adequate method had been developed for the measurement of this motive, progress of a scientific sort had been negligible. The pioneering work of Atkinson and McClelland has provided the basis for the large and very significant body of information that we now possess on this topic. Once a solid, empirical, quantitative foundation of this kind has been laid, the superstructure of concept and data follows rapidly. In a short two decades we see the development of systematic studies of achievement ranging from experimental investigations of risk-taking in the laboratory to the nature of career aspirations in schoolchildren, and to the growth of the economies of underdeveloped nations.

In this volume, Dr. Heckhausen has presented a comprehensive account of the empirical investigations that have been conducted on achievement motivation in many parts of the world. Given the extent of the work to be reported and its significance to psychology, this alone would recommend it highly to any professional reader. Dr. Heckhausen has gone further than this; he presents also an integrated account of the theoretical implications of the data both for a theory of achievement motivation in particular and for theories of motivation in general.

Originally intended for publication in *Progress in Experimental Personality Research,* it became apparent that the scope and extensiveness of the work demanded the production of a separate volume. Translation into English from the German was made by David C. McClelland, Robert C. Birney and Kay F. Butler. For their painstaking care in making this translation we are deeply indebted. We are proud to present this book to the reader as the first of a series of such monographs in the psychology of personality.

Brendan A. Maher

ACKNOWLEDGMENTS

This volume is an extended and revised version of a review article "Leistungsmotivation," published in H. Thomae (Ed.), *Handbuch der Psychologie*, Vol. 2 (Göttingen: Hogrefe, 1965. Pp. 602–702).

The author thanks the publisher, Dr. H. J. Hogrefe, for permission to publish this translated version of the original article. He expresses his gratitude to the translators, Mrs. K. F. Butler, Dr. R. C. Birney, and Dr. D. C. McClelland, for their painstaking efforts and many valuable comments.

The author is also indebted to the editor, Dr. B. A. Maher, for his encouraging interest.

H. Heckhausen

CONTENTS

ABBREVIATIONS

AAT   Achievement Anxiety Test (Alpert & Haber, 1960)

AM   achievement motivation = Leistungsmotivation (measured by the procedure of Heckhausen, (1963) employing the following values:

        HS hope of success = Hoffnung auf Erfolg

        FF   fear of failure = Furcht vor Misserfolg

        NH net hope = Netto-Hoffnung, HS − FF

        TM Total motivation = Gesamtmotivation, HS + FF

CPI   California Psychological Inventory

EPPS Edwards Personal Preference Schedule

FTI   French Test of Insight (French, 1955, 1958a)

IPIT   Iowa Picture Interpretation Test (Hurley, 1955)

MAS Manifest Anxiety Scale (Taylor, 1953)

n Ach need achievement (measured by the procedure of McClelland et al., 1953)

TAQ Test Anxiety Questionnaire (Mandler & Sarason, 1952)

TAT   Thematic Apperception Test

The Anatomy of
Achievement Motivation

CHAPTER I

INTRODUCTION

Problems in the psychology of motivation transcend the traditional boundaries that separate psychic functions such as perception, memory, thinking, and learning. These problems suggest a greater interconnectedness of these functions than seems apparent from the variety of psychic phenomena they represent. Furthermore, the psychology of motivation has become increasingly experimental. Research on achievement motivation in the past decade, as will be summarized, is clear evidence of this fact.

The motivation of achievement-related behavior obviously deserves attention. On the one hand, it has historical connections with research on motivation conducted by two pioneers in German psychology—namely, Narziss Ach (1910) and Kurt Lewin (1926).[1] The former attempted to explain the achievement-related behavior of subjects in his laboratory utilizing the concept of "determining tendency," the latter employing the concept of "quasi-need." On the other hand, psychological experimenters and testers have relied on no other motive to the extent which they have relied on achievement motivation to keep their subjects responding. Yet they

---

[1] When Boring, the historian of our discipline, years ago ran into the nowadays quite familiar abbreviation for achievement motivation, "n Ach" (need Achievement), he asked himself what it could have to do with N(arziss) Ach!

1

induce it without having any control over its effects, properly speaking. Nor are they able to take into account individual differences in achievement motivation, despite the obvious fact that these differences must exist. Instead the experimenter or tester must assume that they are insignificant or that he has somehow eliminated them entirely as variables that will influence the behavior of his subjects.

It is for this reason that the method of measuring achievement motivation developed by the research group of David C. McClelland represents a "breakthrough" which is significant for future work in psychology that goes beyond the narrow area of achievement motivation itself (McClelland, Atkinson, Clark, & Lowell, 1953; Atkinson, 1958; cf. the summary by Birney, in press). This volume is based largely on findings obtained with this and similar methods of measuring motivation. In this volume also an attempt will be made to arrange the findings in terms of a theoretical framework although such an attempt must obviously be regarded as provisional if not premature.

A theory of *motivation,* as provided by the author (Heckhausen, 1963a), cannot be presented here; however, it should be noted that motivation is not to be understood as a final causal element as it may be in common-sense psychology; rather the term refers to the interaction dynamics of many factors in a given person-environment relationship involving goal-directed experience and behavior. Potential and actual motivation should be differentiated.[2] Potential motivation is a normative state which determines, as does a frame of reference, how (in relation to the self) a given category of life situations has to be constituted to be satisfactory for a certain person. Actual motivation (or an aroused motive) consists of

---

[2] Potential motivation is substantially what Atkinson means by the term "motive" while actual motivation is what he means by "motivation" or, in his last publications, by "tendency."

an expectation linking present and future states of being. The strength of the motive arousal corresponds to the steepness of the expectation gradient which is determined (1) by the size of the discrepancy between the present and future states of being within the frame of reference of the normative motivational state, and (2) by the psychic distance between the states of being over time.

From this point of view it is also useful to distinguish between normative and situational states of motivation because the *same strength* of motivation in different people may be traced to *different* normative states in combination with different aroused states of motivation. Furthermore, *different strengths* of motivation may also be based on the *same* normative states in combination with different states of arousal. For intra- as well as interindividual comparisons one ought to isolate or at least control normative as well as aroused states – that is, the lasting as well as the situationally specific components of motivation. Greater attention is usually focused on the normative state as a personality characteristic of importance: the experimenter can control arousal conditions and can try, at least externally, either to keep them constant or to vary them systematically.

However, how is he to isolate the normative motivational state with its evaluative dispositions (Young, 1959), which by definition cannot be manipulated or varied on a short-term basis? Findings to be reported here are based mainly on the not unfounded opinion that the Thematic Apperception Test (TAT) method is, however crude, suitable for measuring motivation. But motivation in the sense of the normative state of a category of person-environment relationships cannot be isolated directly or in its essence even with the TAT. In order to become manifest, potential motivation needs situational arousal. Therefore, the strength and kind of potential motivation with its respective evaluative dispositions can best be revealed only when motivation is activated, i.e., aroused under standardized conditions. This general consideration permits the deduction that an important preliminary condition for the isolation of potential motivation is to find those conditions of arousal under which the dispositional aspects can best find their expression. Questions of this kind have become of basic theoretical importance (cf. Atkinson, 1958a,b; Epstein, 1962; Heckhausen, 1964a).

In this volume we concern ourselves only with a special category of person-environment relationships which may be considered as involving an achievement theme. This content area comprises everything that represents "a competition with a standard of excellence" (McClelland *et al.*, 1953). Something like this is present when a performance, its outcome or the capacity to produce it, is viewed, experienced, or judged within a frame of reference consisting of a more or less gradual slope of "better" or "worse." This frame of reference is defined in terms of various standards of excellence which vary on a dimension of abstractness–generality versus concreteness –specificity. In its simplest form the standard of excellence represents a classification of alternatives: passed–failed; good–bad. Frequently such a classification is used only in an undeveloped early phase, for standards of excellence can differentiate extraordinarily if a certain environmental relationship remains achievement-oriented over a long period of time. The developmental psychology of such standards of excellence has not yet been investigated; they may involve gradients of a nominal, rank or interval scale, and one or more intricately connected dimensions of judgment (cf. Crandall, Preston, & Rabson, 1960b). Moreover, standards of excellence may be task-related (e.g., degree of perfection as the result of performance), or self-related (e.g., comparison with one's own earlier achievements), or other-related (e.g., comparison with the achievement of others, for example in competition). *Achievement motivation* can, therefore, be defined as the striving to increase, or keep as high as possible, one's own capability in all activities in which a standard of excellence is thought to apply and where the execution of such activities can, therefore, either succeed or fail.

In the final analysis, success and failure are always incidents relevant to an achievement-oriented person-environment relationship and thus are transient terminal states related to achievement motivation. No matter how differentiated a standard of excellence may be, it consists of one part which signifies success (no matter how strong), and another which signifies failure; the parts are separated by a more or less narrow boundary area if not a boundary line. Depending on the achievement obtained, this boundary line moves up or down and with it the objective zero point. Therefore it is not possible to define *objectively* for a *long period* which incident in an individual case will signify success and which will signify failure. A completely different question involves a change in structure of the standard of excellence itself. Thus, for example, as with any other frame of reference, the number of steps and their level can change in time.

From the research on the level of aspiration (Hoppe, 1930) we have known that successes and failures occur only within an area of medium difficulty; achieving something that is too easy is not experienced as success, and failing at something too difficult is not experienced as failure. If it is progressively easier to reach a goal, then the achievement-related incentive dwindles until it finally disappears, although the external environmental relationship remains unchanged. The same thing happens if something turns out to be unattainable.

Success and failure occur also in person-environment relationships that have nothing to do with achievement. For the sake of brevity, success and failure will only be used in an achievement-oriented sense in what follows. Achievement themas center around either the possibility of arriving at success or of avoiding failure. Correspondingly, there is an approach or avoidance tendency in achievement motivation:

"Hope of Success" and "Fear of Failure" (cf. Chapter III, Evaluative Dispositions; also McClelland, 1951; Mowrer, 1960).

CHAPTER II

CONTENT ANALYSIS

There is no question that the measurement of individual differences allows deeper insight into the functional dynamics of motivation than has been possible until now on the basis of previously used methods in this area. These other methods have consisted mainly of variations in (*a*) task requirements and (*b*) criteria for selecting groups of subjects (criterion group analysis).

I. EARLY RESEARCH

As early as 1938 Murray and his collaborators tried with their pioneering book, *Explorations in Personality,* not only to define need Achievement but also to obtain individual differences in motive strength by means of a questionnaire. Using a six-part scale, the subject was asked to agree to, or reject, ten (somewhat crude) achievement-oriented statements. This questionnaire (DeCharms, Morrison, Reitman & McClelland, 1955) as well as an improved one similar to the Edwards Personal Preference Schedule (EPPS, A. L. Edwards, 1954; cf. footnote p. 131) seem to isolate motivational variables less than general culture-dependent valuations of achievement abilities and the like which are desirable but not necessarily obligatory for oneself. At any rate, these questionnaire data show very little correlation with behavior in which competition with some standard of excellence is expressed; this is in contrast to content analytic procedures that utilize the TAT method, which so far have shown no correlation worth mentioning with the questionnaire data that provide more or less direct self-judgments (cf. McClelland, 1958d; Marlowe, 1959). It is obvious that one must become detached from what constitutes the obvious (or culture-bound) frame of reference of personal experience if he is to get at dispositions that evaluate the self in all its achievement-oriented activities in relation to the environment.

Nevertheless, it would be premature to consider question-naire methods as basically unsuitable for measuring motivation. Using very carefully selected items for various achievement-oriented responses, Vukovich, Heckhausen, and von Hatzfeld (1964) have found a number of relations with Heckhausen's TAT measure (1963b) of achievement motivation. Interestingly, this is especially the case when the questionnaire items do not refer to an obvious sociocultural evaluative norm. For instance, such a norm does not unambiguously lead to a preference for short term versus long term goals. And only preference for the latter correlates with TAT n Achievement. A cross-validation of this work has yet to be done. Questionnaire schedules such as the "Achievement Anxiety Test" (AAT; Alpert & Haber, 1960; Dember, Nairne, & Miller, 1962; Milholland, 1964), or the one based on the "California Psychological Inventory" by Gough (CPI, 1957, 1964) have proved to be promising in the prediction of academic achievement. Recently, Carney (1964a,b, 1965) has reported significant correlations between the TAT measure (n Ach) and a questionnaire index ("Achievement Orientation"), which he has composed from some scales of the CPI. Since the TAT measure has proved to be much more sensitive to situational factors on tested college groups (factors such as the prevailing motivation of the instructor, manner of the social interaction in the teaching situation, and different courses), the level of the correlations obtained vacillates considerably with such changes in testing conditions. Interestingly, the scores on Carney's questionnaire rise if the achievement-oriented degree of arousal is stepped up in the test instructions — an effect which has also been used to validate the TAT measure.

Ratings by others as well as experimentally obtained performance data have not yielded up to now a conclusive assessment of achievement motivation (cf. for details McClelland, 1958d). The difficulty with ratings by others is obtaining reasonable and general agreement on the behaviors that are valid indicators of the motive in question. It is easy to forget that performance is always a complex result of many other personality-specific factors like ability, skill, cognitive functioning, belief systems based on previous experience, etc. In addition to these factors, differences in potential motivation are evened out in their effect on actual performance under the pronounced arousal conditions of an achievement test situation.

Eysenck (1960) has proposed measuring the strength of motivation with the aid of the size of the reminiscence phenomenon observed after a pause interpolated during the massed practice of an activity. His findings, however, are inconclusive (cf. pp. 115f.).

II. THEORY OF THE THEMATIC APPERCEPTION METHOD

In contrast with other methods cited, the strategy of the TAT method of content analysis employs three tactics in order to enter the hitherto impregnable fortress of differences in motivation potential. (1) The subject remains unaware of the true aim of the test. In contrast to methods using self-ratings, factors such as self-consciousness, self-deception, glossing over, and "folk-psychological" bias play a minor role. (2) The inner motives of experience and behavior are "tapped" in the fantasy stories rather close to the source before they become less recognizable because of a number of further psychological factors and external reasons which all affect their final manifestation in behavior. The preference for fantasy content versus overt behavior (whether obtained through ratings by others or through performance) as a means of uncovering hidden motives can be traced to a revolutionary idea introduced by Freud (1900). (3) The TAT method allows a wide latitude within which person-environment relationships, referred to in the material produced under aroused conditions can be apperceived and elaborated in a most individual manner. Thus it is possible to record an abundance of experiences, courses of action, events, interpersonal interactions, etc. such as will rarely be observed in reality, much less in laboratory experiments, in such an economical way; to say nothing of the difficulties of scrutinizing and isolating actual behavior and experience on an individually comparable basis.

As already mentioned, potential motivation, if it operates like a frame of reference of a normative state, can be isolated only indirectly via situational arousal. If the achievement-oriented content of the projected TAT picture is unmistakable, it elicits a conception of an achievement-related person-environment relationship, i.e., an objective state of arousal. The latter will create in the subject a personality-specific discrepancy with his own normative state (evaluative disposition). This discrepancy will be expressed, depending on its size, in differing strengths in the formulated stories. If the discrepancy, for example, is very great (and therefore its corresponding expectation gradient), the story-teller will describe the people as performing and experiencing in more varied and explicit ways before he ends the achievement-oriented action in a way appearing significant to himself. (Compare Atkinson, 1958b; also the Theory of Conditioned Motive Arousal by Fuchs, 1954, 1963; also Kornadt, 1963). If the discrepancy is not so great, the story will be achievement-related, but perfunctory.

This account of the test process is, of course, at best a theoretical simplification. Thus, for example, the determinant of the discrepancy which leads the storyteller to a characteristic expectation gradient, namely the cue value of the picture, is not constant across persons although the objectively identical picture is shown to all story-tellers (Atkinson, 1958b). The dispersion thus caused, however, does not necessarily have to be error variance insofar as the cue value itself probably depends on the person's normative evaluative disposition. The most obvious hypothesis is that the picture content in combination with the action in the stories told arouses a discrepancy between the normative and the actual which would also be more or less characteristic for situations which belong to the same content category in the storyteller's real life.

However, things do not appear to be this simple. According to the latest results of a representative sample of American men as reported in a field study by Veroff, Feld, and Crockett (1965), more valid motivation scores are obtained from stories to pictures which differ from the everyday work environment. Thus, pictures of blue collar situations yield n Ach scores which predict indices of social status mobility best for subjects from white collar occupations, and vice versa, white collar pictures work better for blue collar workers. Perhaps it is possible that pictures of one's own professional environment are more likely to elicit banal stories involving everyday routines. On the other hand, there are also paradoxical effects of arousal as, for instance, found by Meyer, Heckhausen, and Kemmler (1965). A small subgroup provided more success imagery to failure-oriented pictures and more failure imagery to success-oriented pictures than did the rest of the subject population. Since this subgroup consisted mainly of borderline students, and on the whole shows a much greater fear-of-failure, the paradox of the reversed relationship can be explained as an avoidance reaction triggered by the picture cues.

For reasons of efficiency, achievement-oriented arousal should be for the most part moderate and should apply only to the picture content and not to instructions, pretesting, etc. If the arousal is too intense (i.e. if the subject is pressed for achievement from all sides), individual differences in the characteristic discrepancy between normative and actual states are leveled out which means favoring intraindividual variance, based on the situation, at the expense of interindividual variance, based on normative evaluative dispositions. Actually, it has been shown that the discriminative power of the TAT method is best under neutral test conditions and with pictures of moderate achievement cue value [McClelland *et al.*, 1953; Haber & Alpert, 1958; cf. Heckhausen, critique (1964a) of a study by Schubert-Jäckel & Mehl, 1962)]. If there has been previous strong arousal through instructions, a weak picture arousal will discriminate better than a strong one (Murstein, 1963). It should be remembered that most situations for which one wants to make predictions about performance, are neutral, i.e. task-oriented. French (1955b) has shown that the measurement of motivation under task-oriented conditions has the highest correlation with later measurements of motivation and performance made under the same task-oriented test conditions. Moreover, extremely strong arousal may activate defenses and avoidance tendencies, as was found by McClelland *et al.* (1953, p. 103), Scott (1956; see below p. 57), and Anderson (1962) for achievement motivation as well as for other motives (cf. Epstein, 1962). On the other hand, there are no advantages in weakening the achievement cue value of the picture to the point at which it could mean anything; the apperceptive response competition thus provoked could only be useful if one wanted to obtain the intraindividual characteristic profile of *various* motivations.

There have been attempts to prove that the production in fantasy of achievement-oriented stories does not give any direct information about the achievement orientation of actual behavior but rather plays a compensatory or substitute role. That is, a person who cannot attain his goals in real life will produce stories with a distinct achievement-related content, and vice versa (Lazarus, Baker, Broverman, & Mayer, 1957; Lazarus, 1961; Vogel, Baker, & Lazarus, 1958; Vogel, Raymond, & Lazarus, 1959). The works cited are isolated cases and should be viewed with caution since their measurement of achievement motivation with the TAT has been found to be defective (cf. Atkinson, 1961; Heckhausen, 1963b) or is even lacking (Broverman, Jordan, & Phillips, 1960). According to present knowledge a direct relationship between achievement motivation and TAT content may be considered an established fact; this relationship, however, can be obliterated, or even reversed, under nonoptimal arousal conditions in the TAT process. A reversal is not based on a compensatory or substitute mechanism but rather reflects directly *situationally aroused* inhibitory tendencies which are connected with the motives evoked. An example has been furnished (see also Scott, 1956), as already mentioned, in the paradoxical effects of arousal on success and failure pictures among so-called fear-of-failure subjects. A further finding by Meyer *et al.* (1965) should also be mentioned here in which poor pupils produced less failure content with failure pictures than good pupils although the contrary had to be expected on the basis of school records of both groups. More distinct reversed relationships can be found with motives whose expression is controlled by social norms, as is especially the case with the sexual motive (cf. Clark & Sensibar, 1955) and with aggression (cf. Lesser, 1958). In such instances the TAT content decreases with increased arousal. Even with motives of neutral value, such as the need for food and sleep, over-arousal will yield reversal effects which Epstein (1962) quite convincingly interpreted as "reality-oriented inhibition" in the service of the carrying out the task requirements.

III. EXPERIMENTAL METHOD

Four to six pictures (cf. Atkinson, 1958c) are normally used in a group test. An effort is made to achieve a neutral or a slightly relaxed atmosphere; and prior achievement tests ought not to be conducted under any circumstances. A picture is projected for about 20 seconds; then the following four questions are answered on prepared forms: What is happening? What has led up to the situation? What are the people thinking and feeling? What will be the outcome? About 1 minute is allowed for each question. The evaluation of the stories is accomplished by means of a scoring key that determines which statements fall into various content categories and, therefore, are to be scored as points that finally are totaled to provide a final score for all the stories written by a subject. Aside from the pictures used and the standardized test conditions, the scoring key is the most important part of the method that has been tested and validated.

The scoring key was developed originally by McClelland, Atkinson, Clark, and Lowell (1953); the work cited describes the key and discusses in detail its development and validation. The best reference for details on the scoring key is Atkinson (1958c) in which a special self-study course in the use of scoring system is found. With the help of the scoring key, one may determine whether the story is achievement-oriented at all (e.g., whether it contains some reference to competition with a standard of excellence or statements about a long-term achievement goal). If this is the case, various content areas in the story can be scored (once each): for instance, Need (or goal setting); Instrumental Activity; Positive and Negative Affective States; Goal Anticipation, and other areas. Scores derived in this original procedure as set out by McClelland and co-workers will be called *n* Ach (need Achievement)[3] in this volume.

Another related measure is provided by the French "Test of Insight" (FTI), developed by Elizabeth French (1955b, 1958b). It consists of ten short statements about what certain people do, desire, or fear. The subjects are asked to give a reason for these statements and to write it down. Coding of the response is done with a scoring key similar to that for the *n* Ach measure. Validation studies have confirmed a good agreement between the two methods (French & Thomas, 1958; Atkinson & Litwin, 1960).[4] A combination of projective technique and multiple-choice test characterizes the "Iowa Picture Interpretation Test" (IPIT; Hurley, 1955, 1957; Johnston, 1957). The subject is to choose among several complete stories for each picture; one of the stories is achievement-oriented. It is still questionable whether it is possible to obtain something similar to the *n* Ach measure with this method (cf. Williams, 1955; McClelland, 1958d, p. 39; Barnette, 1961). Aronson (1958) developed a nonverbal measure which is based on distinctions in the graphic structure of simple psychomotor formations (doodles). Up to the present time this has been mainly used with children and in cross-cultural comparisons (McClelland, 1961). Finally, Knapp (1958) found certain color preferences, and Morgan (1964) the range of incentive values assigned to easy and difficult occupations, to be indexes of *n* Ach.

---

[3] In what follows, if results of non-German authors are reported, achievement motivation has usually been measured with the *n* Ach score unless otherwise stated.

[4] On the other hand, Himelstein, Eschenbach, and Carp (1958) reported a zero correlation between the two methods, but they did not report on the testing conditions in detail.

The scoring key of the n Ach measure does not differentiate between the tendencies to achieve success and to avoid failure. This differentiation has shown itself to be of importance quite early in correlating n Ach scores with certain criterion variables (McArthur, 1953; R. W. Brown, 1953; Scott, 1956; Clark, Teevan, & Ricciuti, 1956; Ricciuti & Schultz, 1954), e.g., with the recognition threshold for words (McClelland & Liberman, 1949), the recall of finished and unfinished tasks (Atkinson, 1953), and of success and failure-related stories (Reitman, 1961). According to these studies, failure-avoidant tendencies are accompanied by low to medium n Ach scores. Cooper and Howell (1961) have not found any relationship in this range of n Ach scores with test symptoms of neurotic tendencies. From this they conclude that failure avoidance is an independent dimension and not necessarily the obverse of a success-seeking tendency (cf. Reitman & Williams, 1961).

Starting from the recall findings obtained by Atkinson (1953), Moulton (1958) attempted a separation of these tendencies via content analysis, employing a system that has not been used since except by Hoyos (1965). Instead, more use has been made in recent studies of anxiety questionnaires to assess the failure-oriented aspect of achievement motivation. The "Test Anxiety Questionnaire" (TAQ, Mandler & Sarason, 1952) appears to differentiate better than the unspecific "Manifest Anxiety Scale" (MAS, Taylor, 1953); this seems to be true also for the more recent "Achievement Anxiety Test" (AAT, Alpert & Haber, 1960; see also Dember et al., 1962).

Starting with the n Ach key, Heckhausen (1963b) has developed and validated two new keys for "Hope of Success" and "Fear of Failure" for a six-picture series. The two dimensions of story content do not correlate with each other. In what follows they will be abbreviated into HS motivation and FF motivation, and the sum of the two will be called total, or combined, motivation. N Ach correlates between +.40 and

+.70 with HS and HS + FF motivation, but not significantly with FF motivation. Meyer *et al.* (1965), borrowing from Heckhausen's method, have developed and successfully validated an age-specific series of pictures and an individual testing method for children of elementary school age. Hoyos (1965), following Moulton (1958), has also devised two keys for the two tendencies. Birney, Burdick, and Teevan (1961) have developed a key for "Hostile Press" which is thought to be an equivalent of fear of failure. However, this takes into account not only achievement-oriented content but every threat theme involving the main protagonists in the TAT stories.

IV. VALIDATION

Validation of content analysis of motivation can be carried out in two different ways. First, one can consider intraindividual differences which appear through the planned variation in arousal conditions of the motive being measured. This has mainly been done by McClelland *et al.* (1953) and Hayashi and Habu (1962a, 1962b). They found that achievement-related statements increase significantly if the achievement arousal rises from a "relaxed-casual" to a "neutral" to an "ego-involved" test instruction. Second, one can consider interindividual differences and correlate the scores obtained with behavioral measures which appear to be validation criteria. The latter approach was used by Heckhausen (1963b) in the differentiation and scoring of the two motivational tendencies, HS and FF. Validating findings of this kind for the different methods of scoring will be mentioned frequently in the following sections.

When arousal conditions are increased, American college co-eds in contrast to their male fellow students strangely enough do not show any increase in *n* Ach scores (McClelland *et al.*, 1953) since they apparently have already been strongly achievement-aroused under neutral conditions (Veroff *et al.*, 1953). According to other findings it is possible to stimulate achievement thoughts among college women if success is related to "social acceptability" (McClelland, 1958a). Findings with Brazilian (Angelini, 1959), Japanese (Hayashi & Habu, 1962a), and German female students (Heckhausen, 1963b) have not given reason to conclude that the method is differentially valid for the two sexes. The differences are perhaps the result of widely varying methods of selecting "random" samples. Compared with women undergraduates in the United States, those in Brazil, Japan, and Germany constitute a selected minority whose achievement-oriented self-concept is closer to that of the male sex. Lesser, Krawitz, and Packard (1963) have measured the *n* Ach of under- and over-achieving college students of the same intelligence level under neutral and ego-involved arousal conditions. The over-achieving college women showed the expected increase in *n* Ach scores only with TAT pictures depicting females, whereas the under-achievers showed an increase in *n* Ach only to pictures of males. It can be seen that only the former consider achievement capability to be a part of their female role; the latter, however, consider this to be a male attribute.[5]

French and Lesser (1964) have pursued this finding and selected women undergraduates according to whether their preference was for intellectual or social-domestic excellence, i.e., whether their achievement orientation corresponded to the male or female role concept. When the preferred value orientation was for the "male role," they obtained the expected increase in *n* Ach scores under ego-involved testing conditions. In contrast, according to Lesser *et al.* (1963), it is not

---

[5] Female "college leaders," however, obtain higher *n* Ach scores in stories told to a male rather than to a female figure in the picture, as Alper (1957) reports.

very critical whether stories are composed to male or female cues (here in the FTI) even though male cues.combined with intellectual value orientations and female cues combined with social-domestic value orientations do lead to a some-what greater increase in the n Ach scores. If the validation criterion does not consist of an increase in n Ach scores but of a correlation with performance on an intellectual achievement task after arousal of an intellectual value orientation, the same relationships appear as found by Lesser *et al.* in the earlier study (1963). In a female group with intellectual ("male") value orientation, only those obtaining high n Achievement in stories to female cues actually performed better. Similarly among the women with a social-domestic ("female") value orientation, those who scored high in n Achievement in response to male cues were the ones who performed better. Moss and Kagan (1961; Kagan & Moss, 1962) did not find any sex differences involving the relation-ship of achievement motivation in the TAT and achievement behavior in adults (r_s = +.37 and +.52 respectively). But during adolescence (10–16 years of age), the correlation is negative for girls, particularly with mechanical achievement.

V. RELIABILITY

The coding reliability, i.e., the objectivity of the scoring key, is satisfactory in all the procedures (n Achievement, AM, FTI, IPIT). Scorer agreements between .80 and .90 or better have been reported. The test-retest reliability, how-ever, is less satisfactory. As far as the n Achievement measure is concerned, coefficients as low as +.22 (McClelland, 1955) or +.26 (Krumboltz & Farquhar, 1957) seem to be untrust-worthy estimates, perhaps due to the shortness of the test (three pictures), the use of the same pictures which could have "spoiled" the subjects for the second test, cyclic satiation effects in fantasy productions (Reitman & Atkinson, 1958), or too weak a cue value of the original picture series, etc. At any rate, Haber and Alpert (1958) have found a more satisfactory correlation, +.54 (with an interval of 3 weeks), with two parallel sets of six pictures each, the cue content of which had been carefully equated (see also Birney, 1958a, 1959). In longitudinal studies Kagan and Moss (1959) found a significant coefficient of stability for indices from age 8 years 9 months to 14 years 6 months, and Moss and Kagan (1961) found similar results over a period of 10 years from adolescence into adulthood $(r=+.31)$. In line with these findings are recent ones reported by McClelland (1965b) showing that n Ach scores of college students predict life outcome over periods of 10 years or more. Himelstein and Kimbrough (1960) have reported similar test-retest reliabilities for the FTI measure.

Heckhausen's n Ach method yielded test-retest coefficients between +.40 and +.60 for success (HS) and failure (FF) motivation using the same six pictures after a five-week period. Since the repetition of "projective" methods is subject to various unfavorable effects (cf. McClelland, 1958a; Reitman & Atkinson, 1958; Heckhausen, 1963b), it is possible that the reliability is underestimated rather than overestimated by current findings. The high sensitivity of thematic apperceptive methods to situational factors (e.g., status of the experimenter, Birney, 1958b; cf. Carney, 1964a) validates them in one sense, although it has serious disadvantages psychometrically speaking. The methods are presently not suitable for psychodiagnostic purposes, i.e. for individual diagnosis although their degree of discrimination is sufficient for experimental research.

CHAPTER III

EVALUATIVE DISPOSITIONS (VALUE ATTITUDES)

I. INDICATORS

As has been stated, potential motivation can be described as a pattern of evaluative dispositions involving a certain thema which underlies a normative state. The most general measure would be some sort of estimate of the level of the normative state or, more explicitly, of the mean discrepancy between a normative state and various situational states. Such a measure represents the strength of achievement motivation, i.e. the salience of a tendency to think in terms of competing with a standard of excellence. Martire (1956) was able to show, in fact, that the group with the strongest (as well as most generalized) achievement motivation also produces the greatest discrepancy between real and ideal self-image and between actual and desired possession of achievement-related personal traits. Coopersmith (1959) and Reimanis (1964) found the same to be true using ratings by self and others but in connection with the same type of motivation (the need for Achievement).

Before we continue with the problem of estimating the strength of the general tendency (or the discrepancy between ideal and real), another characteristic of achievement motivation should be discussed: namely, the relative dominance of a success-oriented versus a failure-oriented evaluative

21

disposition. Depending on the weight given the two alternatives of success and failure, the evaluative disposition retains a characteristic center of gravity which is expressed in anticipation as well as in judgment of outcome. Thus "success-motivated" persons, when setting a goal, consider the probability of success rather than that of failure; they judge their levels of achievement against a general background colored with success expectation, and, correspondingly, the reverse is true for failure-motivated persons (Heckhausen, 1963b). In these cases the evaluative dispositions do not operate directly as directional tendencies but indirectly as frames of reference which are not the result of immediate experience but which influence the outcome of goal setting or judgment.

Moreover, it has been possible to observe more generalized effects of success- and failure-oriented evaluative dispositions which do not have an immediately obvious connection with success and failure. They show, for instance, characteristic differences in the structure and quality of time experience with respect to such characteristics as future time span or the goal-directedness and speed of passage of experienced time (cf. p. 41). Finally, even content-free perception seems to be influenced by such evaluative dispositions as, for instance, the shrinking and expanding of lines which are overestimated by success-motivated persons and underestimated by failure-motivated persons, respectively. It can be assumed that this effect depends on a different metric (still another component of the frame of reference) for perception of such differences. To connect such a phenomenon with success and failure in this instance seems to be reasonable only in a metaphorical sense (Heckhausen, 1963b).

Recently there have been more systematic attempts to investigate conceptions of success and failure. In a factor-analytic study of preferences for various metaphors, Knapp and Green (1964) found three dimensions of meaning for success: the radiant, the illusory, and the capricious. Katz

(1964) has shown with adolescents that the meaning of success varies significantly with socioeconomic background. Accumulation of possessions, job security, status position, and personal excellence are all centers of gravity which increase in importance from lower to higher social classes in this order (more about this below, see p. 28). Highly motivated persons (n Ach) attach more importance to excellence than to prestige while the reverse is true with those of low motivation (Burnstein, Moulton, & Liberty, 1963). People who are considered especially "successful" in small American towns have distinguished themselves above all through community activities in organizations and public institutions but less through income, vocation, and level of education (Kaltenbach & Mc-Clelland, 1958). This quasi-public perceived "success" correlates with the achievement motivation (n Ach) of the individuals involved.

Ertel (1964) asked male undergraduates to evaluate an upcoming intelligence test with the help of the Semantic Differential; he found two dimensions that correspond to the effective values characteristic of success and failure expectations. The success-motivated persons (based on HS score) experienced the coming intelligence test predominantly with anticipatory feelings of confidence while the failure-motivated (high FF score) entertained feelings of apprehensiveness. Kassarjian (1963) has distinguished social and self-oriented dimensions of success and failure which correlate with each other. Failure in both dimensions goes hand in hand with various signs of a poor self-concept and difficulty in social affiliations. Cooper and Howell (1961), however, have pointed out that failure motivation (n Ach, middle and lower third of the distribution) does not correlate with neurotic symptoms in behavior. Either of the two tendencies (HS or FF) may be appropriate and healthy or inappropriate and neurotic depending on its prominence relative to the other.

Evaluative dispositions can be further estimated from the particular degree of excellence that is generally preferred, i.e., experienced as proper or even as compulsory, when a person is in competition with a standard of excellence. Such degrees of excellence have been labeled "level of aspiration" since Hoppe (1930) and Dembo (1931). A success-oriented evaluative disposition is not necessarily associated with a high or the highest level of aspiration, nor is a failure-oriented one necessarily associated with the lowest levels of aspiration. There is a group of "failure-motivated" persons who aim at the highest degrees of excellence although they remain far from realizing them. Individual psychology, especially as expounded by Künkel (1928), had such cases in mind when attempting to explain feelings of inferiority and heightened aspiration as opposites which promote each other. Success-motivated Ss experience a degree of excellence as having "demand quality" if it lies above their level of achievement, but only if it is slightly above, so that it can still be reached with a concerted effort. (Compare Chapter VIII.)

Evidently a high degree of generality enables evaluative dispositions to apply to the most diverse situations in the life span (viewed either historically or contemporaneously) so long as some kind of achievement theme can be extracted from them. This has led to the much-discussed phenomenon that one may act in exactly the same way in completely different situations. In order to derive this phenomenon, causal explanations have been constructed which go back to innate drives—as in psychoanalysis—or to secondary acquired drives. J. S. Brown (1953), for example, traces the desire to be active and to earn money back to a fear of scarcity of money which is acquired early by the little child when observing his parents looking worried because of an insufficient family budget.

Allport (1937) has protested against "derivation theory" and has substituted the "principle of the functional autonomy

of motives." His thinking remains, however, within the context of derivation theory; however, in his theory, the causal-
historical links are broken thus producing functional autonomy. It is possible to support his effort to bring out the uniqueness of individual behavior, at least as far as achievement
motivation is concerned, with a simpler construct, i.e., the
transferability of evaluative structures. Thus we should
remember that the evaluative dispositions (normative states)
possess a high degree of generality which favors their transferability (cf. Fuchs, 1954, pp. 66 ff.). This explains certain
developmental events. At a given period of time certain types
of activity begin and others cease to be achievement-
motivated. This cannot occur until the activities have moved
in the course of individual development into the realm of
possible mastery; and, as is known, they no longer remain
achievement-motivated when they have been mastered completely. Therefore, in the course of life it is constantly possible
for new and changing situational constellations to become
achievement-oriented because they have not yet been
mastered. To explain this fact it is not necessary to fall back
on a causal-historical chain of events with or without the
concept of functional autonomy.

The high degree of generality of the evaluative dispositions,
however, does not remove the difficulties which arise in char-
acterizing them in the individual case. How are we to measure
them and to make them comparable across individuals if
they lead in one case, for example, to wishful goal settings
and in another to active instrumental activities if the activities
are short and intense in some people and more enduring in
others? If the achievement theme includes in some people
only a small or in others a large number of person-environment
relationships? Obviously, one would be inclined to consider
an evaluative disposition as more prominent (1) the more it
leads to actions and not just wishful fantasies, (2) the more
it leads to an enduring and not just sporadic activity, and (3)

the more situations of different kinds it manages to organize as related to itself.

Even in considering just these three characteristics, many combinations ought to be taken into account in the individual case; thus it remains crude and problematic to reduce them all to the common denominator of a simple intensity scale for the sake of interindividual comparisons. A systematic investigation of the multidimensional structure of evaluative dispositions is still only in a very early stage. Top priority belongs to the question of the extent to which achievement motivation is generalized or specific. That is, how many and how varied are the person-environment relationships which can be included within the framework of the same evaluative disposition?

II. AREA OF GENERALIZATION

The achievement-related sections of the personal world differ in width from person to person. They depend also on sociocultural and developmental norms which give them a certain uniformity. In certain apparently neurotic cases, the achievement thema may be so "overvalued" that it embraces practically every situational relationship. The area of generalization could be staked out using the TAT method if the pictures presented were to represent well-distributed random samples of the universe of all situational relationships (although this is hardly conceivable). While the clinical application of the TAT is based on this concept (Murray, 1943) in order to determine the prominence of various motives, the standardized content analytic methods try to avoid (for reasons already discussed) apperceptive conflicts as to what is going on. The pictures are chosen to have an unmistakable cue value. The strength of motivation is, therefore, determined less through the extent of generalization of the achievement response to various pictures than through the frequency and salience of achievement-related aspects of the behavioral sequences described.

Therefore, the conclusions reached by this method should be limited to the thematic range of the pictures presented (cf. however, Veroff *et al.*, 1965; above, p. 11). Nevertheless, as Martire (1956) has shown, even a thematically limited series of pictures provides some indication of the degree of generalization of *n* Ach if the stories have been written first under neutral and later under achievement-arousing conditions. Those persons who produce distinct achievement thema not only under arousal conditions but under neutral conditions as well reveal a strong generalized achievement motivation. The achievement-related apperception of a situation should not be viewed so much as a "project" or volitional "act" of the person. Frequently it is the "demand character" of a situation that obtrudes. Thus, certain people and objects of one's own world nearly always possess an achievement-related cue value, e.g., a teacher or a piece of work. The effects of certain sociocultural, already institutionalized, person-environment relationships can be understood better under the concept of role expectation than under the less specific concept of "demand character" (or valence)—for instance, an employee knows that he is perceived by his employer only in terms of what he achieves (cf. Heider, 1958).

The generalization problem faces us more sharply if we raise questions not only about achievement thematization in general but also about the stability of its several evaluative components, such as the preponderance of success or failure orientation or the level of aspiration. Everyday experience demonstrates that a man is more success-oriented in some activities and more failure-oriented in others; furthermore, he may possess levels of aspiration of varying heights. On the other hand, much can be said for hypothesizing a generalized basic structure which is reflected in the most diverse areas.

It is possible that such a hypothesis is more appealing because it simplifies the problem rather than because it is
actually justified. As long as research results are still lacking,
the question of generalization should be treated with caution.
So far there are only the findings from the research on level of
aspiration which have shown that goal settings remain un-
mistakably consistent from task to task despite wide differences in their "demand character" (cf. below, p. 91).

III. SOCIOCULTURAL FRAMES OF REFERENCES AND THEIR CHANGE OVER HISTORICAL TIME

The concrete person-environment relationships in which
evaluative dispositions operate are always fixed in the frames
of reference of a culture or one of its subcultures. In highly
industrialized mass societies "competition with standards
of excellence" represents a dominant theme in public as well
as private life. This competition had, and still has, a decisive
role in the economic rise of present-day industrial nations
(cf. McClelland, 1961, 1964a). Even in so-called primitive
societies one speaks of an achievement thema which, however, may be rather low, as in the case of the Alorese
(Kardiner, 1945). Weak achievement orientation in a culture
does not of course exclude heightened motivation in individual persons, as Dennis (1955) had shown with the example of the Hopi Indians. No matter how variable achievement activities may be in cross-cultural comparisons, competition with a standard of excellence can be recognized
as easily in an Indian tribe hunting game as in middle-class
business activity in our civilization; thus it appears quite
possible to discover activities which are homologous across
cultures.

McClelland and Friedman (1952) as well as Child, Storm,
and Veroff (1958) have determined the level of achievement

motivation in various preliterate cultures on the basis of content analysis of orally transmitted folktales using the *n* Ach scoring key. Among other things, it was found that the level of achievement motivation ascertained in this way correlates with the incidence of "full-time" entrepreneurial activities in various cultures (McClelland, 1961). An intercultural comparison between the United States and Germany was made by McClelland *et al.* (1958b) using high school students. They found differential emphasis on values for individual or group activities, obligations to oneself or to others, and higher achievement motivation among the American students (cf. McClelland, 1964b).

Within *one* culture there are in turn subcultures in which regard to achievement thema represent relatively closed areas of life thus reflecting characteristic evaluative dispositions. This has frequently been demonstrated in the social strata of a Western industrial society like the United States. In contrast with the lower social stratum of the working class, the middle class is characterized more strongly by activist and future-oriented values that are conceived in terms of individual differences in ability (e.g., Leshan, 1952; Reissman, 1953; Kohn, 1959). Even within the middle-class subculture the contrast in evaluative dispositions can be observed between "bureaucratic" and "managerial" circles (Miller & Swanson, 1956). Achievement themes center more around immediate material rewards in the lower social stratum (Hoffman, Mitsos, & Protz, 1958; Zazzo, 1963; F. M. Katz, 1964). Only if monetary rewards have been promised for a task are pupils from this social stratum as motivated (*n* Ach) as their fellow-students from the middle-class who respond more readily only to the instruction to perform a task (Douvan, 1956). Cameron and Storm (1965) have also shown that lower-class children perform as well as middle-class children in a concept-learning task only when a material reward (candy) is provided. Potential or so-called "interiorized" achievement motivation increases with socioeconomic status (Rosen, 1956, 1962b; Douvan & Adelson, 1958; Veroff, Atkinson, Feld, & Gurin, 1960; Littig & Yeracaris, 1963, 1965; Carney & McKeachie, 1963; Nuttall, 1964; Morgan, 1964; see also below: Conditions of Origin and Development).

Rosen (1956) has demonstrated that evaluative dispositions in two social strata differ with respect to the desire of American pupils to continue their education from high school to college. Unlike achievements attained in school, this desire is not connected with the strength of measured achievement motivation (n Ach) but rather with specific achievement-related evaluative dispositions that are found only in the upper social strata, e.g., to stand on one's own feet at an early age, to plan far ahead and pursue one's career goals actively, to continue one's education for many years without earning money. Academic studies with all their implications are still usually beyond the horizon of even the highly motivated pupils from lower social strata (a point of view which should be taken more into account in attempts at "mobilizing talent reserves"). The limits of achievement-related life space seems to play, as we shall see (pp. 131 f.), a mediating role in the interactions between motivation and ability. According to French and Lesser (1964), achievement motivation in American co-eds is tied to differential value orientations of an intellectual versus a socio-domestic kind (see above, p. 18).

In a large representative sample, Veroff et al. (1960) have obtained estimates of achievement motivation levels of various segments of the American population from individual interviews. The following characteristics marked the population groups with higher n Achievement: higher level of education; higher occupational level; early adulthood (especially between 21 and 24 years) as compared to late adulthood (especially above age 55); small-town or rural as compared to large city residence; growing up in a complete family as compared to the loss of parents through death or divorce before the age of 16.

Stimulated by Max Weber's thesis (1904, 1905) on the connection of Protestantism with capitalism and economic growth, repeated investigations have attempted to ascertain whether Protestants show more pronounced achievement motivation than Catholics. It has not been possible to prove this in the present era either in the United States or Germany (McClelland, 1961). Veroff, Feld, and Gurin (1962) found in a representative random sample for the total American population that Catholic males rank second to Jewish males as more highly motivated than Protestant males. This result could be traced chiefly to the group of Catholics of middle age with low incomes and large families. The authors interpret this unexpected finding as due to the stronger arousal of achievement motivation by the strained economic situation of the Catholic father who earns little money and has many children. This is more likely to be true since he is oriented by his education toward concrete goals and not so much toward widely generalized goals as the Protestant might be in the same situation. However, it may also be that it is precisely the concrete evaluative dispositions of middle-aged Catholics with high achievement motivation that causes them to have large families whose adequate care requires upward mobility.

Upward mobility is, in general, especially marked below the middle class. As shown by Crockett (1962), such mobility is connected here—but not in the middle or upper classes—with the strength of the achievement motivation (cf. Minor & Neel, 1958; and Veroff et al., 1965). In a small but highly industrialized northeastern American community, however, Littig and Yeracaris (1965) found achievement motivation related to intergenerational mobility between classes (in terms of the blue-collar–white-collar distinction). Upward or downward occupational mobility is associated with high and low achievement motivation, respectively. This is true for married women, too, when their mobility is linked to their husband's occupation. Socioeconomic class seems to be of more importance for determining n Ach levels—at least today and in America—than religious affiliation or ethnic origin. However, the Jewish population has appeared to possess a remarkably high achievement motivation even in the lowest social strata (Rosen, 1959; Carney & McKeachie, 1963).

The Calvinistic ethic: "to prove one's worth in a completely worldly 'calling' in order to prove one has been selected for eternal salvation" produced an extraordinary spirit of enterprise which had as its goal not the accumulation of capital but rather the successful growth of an enterprise. The key motive in the spirit of enterprise is *not* (contrary to the universally accepted traditional belief) a striving for profit but a high need to achieve, which leads to a preference for calculated rather than speculative risks. Profit does have importance, however, in an instrumental sense as providing a standard of excellence for efficiency within the economic sphere. Groups of managers or executives (especially in commerce) are, even in Communist countries, more highly motivated (n Ach) than comparable groups of professionals, and they prefer more moderate risks in decision-making (cf. McClelland, 1961; Meyer, Walker, & Litwin, 1961). Furthermore it appears that they become managers because of their n Ach since McClelland (1965) has shown that college males with high n Ach are more likely to be found in entrepreneurial business occupations 14 years later than their peers with low n Ach. If the historical Calvinistic frame of reference resulted in an increase of achievement motivation in some population groups, even in whole countries, and thus in a tremendous economic growth in the early capitalistic era, it is to be expected that history will show further examples of change from generation to generation in the amount of achievement motivation and in associated economic growth and decline.

In the search for such historical covariations it has been possible to scan periods of over a thousand years because of the method of content analysis. One can code random samples of surviving literary texts and associate their *n* Ach content with various independent indicators of economic development. This has been done for ancient Greece from 900–100 B.C., for Spain in the late Middle Ages, for England from the Tudor Kings to the industrial revolution, for the United States from 1800–1950, and finally for the Peruvian culture[6] from around 800 B.C. to 700 A.D. (McClelland, 1961). These studies have shown that economic growth has always been preceded by a period of increased achievement motivation, and economic decline by a continuous period of decreasing achievement motivation. High achievement motivation, therefore, precedes economic growth and not vice versa. The increase in achievement motivation itself seems to be almost always the result of religious and philosophical trends which produce a highly motivated next generation via an unintentional new orientation in child training aimed at early independence and accomplishment. (Compare for details McClelland, 1961, and also below, pp. 151 ff.)

Content analysis of primers (from the third and fourth grades) has revealed *n* Achievement changes in more recent and contemporary history. Lambert and Klineberg (1963) found that *n* Achievement levels so determined correlated

---

[6] Since insufficient written material is available, designs on grave urns were classified on the basis of their achievement-related content, using Aronson's (1958) method. This had previously been used successfully with ancient Greek vases as a method of measuring *n* Ach which paralleled content analysis of literary texts (McClelland, 1958c).

with boys' occupational aspirations in various countries. The method has been applied to longitudinal time series within a given country (America, 1800–1950; DeCharms & Moeller, 1962) as well as to international comparisons of a broad range of capitalistic, communist, and developing countries (McClelland, 1961). DeCharms and Moeller (1962) used as an indicator of economic growth the number of yearly patent registrations per million inhabitants. For his international comparisons, McClelland (1961) used the increase in national income per capita and also the average rate of increase in per capita kilowatt hours of electricity consumed. For an estimate of motivational level he used the achievement-related content of school text books from around 1925 and again around 1950. He found significant correlations of around +.50 between n Achievement in children's readers in one generation and rate of economic growth in the next (or over an even shorter period). It is noteworthy that the achievement motivation of particular countries changed between 1925 and 1950 in a way which has forecast changes in rate of economic development in those countries. Incidentally, it proved to be a methodological stroke of genius to use stories in children's readers as material for content analysis, for they are obviously the condensed reflection of the national *Zeitgeist* as filtered through the minds of pedagogues, yet they are still free of political ideology, at least for these early years.

Poffenberger and Norton (1963) believe that the American public reaction to the Russian "Sputnik Challenge" has already led to an intensification of achievement motivation in male pupils because of the increased interest in mathematics and in achievement in this subject between 1955 and 1960.

IV. VALUE SYSTEMS AND SUBSYSTEMS

An achievement-related evaluative disposition is frequently, if not always, functionally imbedded in overlapping value systems which are, under certain circumstances, rather heterogenous. There are systems that prevent achievement from moving out of an interest in itself into a merely instrumental activity. The phenomenon of the "Protestant Ethic" according to Max Weber (1904, 1905) represents a value system which might be called a religious "superiority complex." Mierke (1955) has shown that through an appeal to urgent worthwhile motives (for the honor of the group and the advancement of science) "super achievements," beyond those established in competitive records, can be reached even in the psychological laboratory.

No doubt there are also temporary or enduring networks of evaluative dispositions that are not intrinsically closely related; for example, if competition with a standard of excellence is in the service of motives for gain or power. In such cases achievement motivation has to be considered as a secondary, i.e. instrumental, system of motivation. Experience and action correlates are so altered in consequence that it is better to distinguish phenomena of this kind from "pure achievement motivation." One can also observe this difference in variations in the arousal conditions under which a task is performed. If the experimenter asks the Ss to cooperate and please him, their performance does not correlate any longer with n Ach but with the social "need for affiliation" (scored similarly with the TAT method, Shipley & Veroff, 1952; cf. French, 1955b; Atkinson & Reitman, 1956; Atkinson & Raphelson, 1956). In addition, achievement motivation no longer shows any connection with performance if it is rewarded with money (Atkinson & Reitman, 1956), or with an hour of free time (French, 1955b).

German studies of character (for instance, Lersch, 1938) tend to conclude that one may under certain circumstances aspire to good performance "only" for the sake of social esteem and prestige. Except in extreme cases, this seems to be less a question of a value system extrinsically connected with achievement, but rather a system in which the achievement thema is typically embedded. A *pure* task orientation is probably a special case as opposed to situations that involve the value or respect one places on himself or which is attributed to him by relevant others. Many achievement goals can in the last analysis be reached only through a social process (Mahler, 1933); that is, it is necessary to inform the relevant people concerned of the achievement result attained before the task has been completed and the goal realized. The difference between a striving for achievement and for esteem can be exaggerated, if one mistakes two reference points for two mutually exclusive kinds of motives. As a rule, goals involving task performance, self-esteem, and social recognition appear side by side. They release each other during the course of the achievement-related experience (even though personality-specific centers of gravity do exist corresponding to these three points of reference). It can hardly be otherwise considering the importance of achievement for social evaluation and professional advancement in our culture.

One can also find authors who have focused on one type of goal or the other. While Wertheimer (1957) and Metzger (1962) attempt to consider the objective demands of a task for educational reasons, Gottschaldt (1933) regards the origin of achievement motivation to lie in the "striving for social prestige." Crandall *et al.* (1960) do not even consider whether strivings might occur for the sake of achievement alone. Rather their definition includes behavior which is directed at "the attainment of approval or avoidance of disapproval" (!) in competition with a standard of excellence. The longitudinal investigations by Kagan and Moss (1962) provide a clear answer to this problem. Achievement behavior for its own sake or for reasons of social esteem correlate so highly that the feasibility of maintaining such a distinction is questionable (cf. pp. 149 ff.), at least insofar as the perception of others is concerned.

CHAPTER IV

IMPORTANT DIMENSIONS
OF EXPERIENCE

I. FOCUS OF THE PERSON-ENVIRONMENT
RELATIONSHIP

The focus of the perception of a situation may be on the self
or on the surrounding world either in its interpersonal or
task-oriented aspects. The latter involves the concern for the
task and the fulfillment of its demands—a concern which can
arise not only from forgetting the self but also from strong ego
involvement in the task.

If the focus of perception is social, it centers on those
effects which one's actions produce in the interpersonal
situation. When the focus is on the self, the course of action
is experienced as a measure of one's own competence or incompetence. Instead of yielding to the temptation of enlarg-
ing on these typologies, it should be pointed out again that the
focus changes normally in a quite unrestricted way. It depends, for instance, on the point reached in the course of
action. For example, the point of reference is more apt to
become social after completion of the task.

It is also of importance whether the type of task involved
necessitates competition with a standard of excellence that is
derived mainly from the task itself, or from one's relations to
others or to oneself. Socially oriented standards of excellence
are always applicable in competition although others may

39

arise as well. In particular, self-oriented standards are also apt to be present in competition. The developmental history of achievement-related perceptions deserves special attention. For instance, 2- to 3-year-olds do not interpret the thwarting of their efforts as failure in the sense of personal inability (i.e., as related to the person or self-esteem) but as resistance of the task, and therefore as related to the task or environment. (More details are given on pp. 143 ff.)

The focus of the perception of the total situation also influences behavior and its effects. An example of the importance of focus lies in the frequently found reversal of the Zeigarnik effect when performance is not task-oriented but self-oriented. In the latter case it is not the incompleted tasks but rather the completed tasks which are best remembered (cf., for instance, Lewis & Franklin, 1944, and Green, 1963). Another similar example is furnished by Silverman (1964): persons with high self-esteem recall fewer facts relating to incompleted tasks after failure than persons with low self-esteem. A finding by Mierke (1955, p. 222 ff.) is notable in this respect. Subjects were alternately shown two different types of tasks of the same basic nature. They were told that they had to solve one set of tasks but that the other set was voluntary. The required tasks were solved faster, albeit more incorrectly, than the voluntary ones. This would seem to be the result of different ways of focusing on or conceptualizing performance. The required tasks evoked self-esteem and a social focus, and the optional tasks a task focus; thus the former led to a predominant interest in a swift solution, and the latter to an interest in a correct solution. Surprisingly, the different conceptualizations of the two tasks carried over into a subsequent performance test *under time pressure;* in fact they contrasted even more sharply. Thus the interest in the voluntary task can be maintained despite pressure now imposed from without!

Occasionally foci in the area of achievement have been referred to as task attitudes which may be task- or ego-oriented (cf. Heckhausen, 1955). It seems more appropriate to define task attitudes simply as specific styles of action which are characteristic for success and failure-oriented evaluative dispositions no matter what kind of focus is present. Thus a success-oriented task attitude favors a quick-moving, concentrated solution process while a failure-oriented attitude leads to tensions, blocking, interpolated inhibitions, and interruptions in carrying out the task. Depending on the type of task, this may be to the benefit or detriment of the achievement outcome (compare Chapters IX and XI).

II. TIME PERSPECTIVE AND THE NATURE OF THE EXPERIENCE OF TIME

Under the experience of time we mean to include the time-related aspects of all the experiences of a person which, at a certain period in the present, reach into the future and go back into the past (L. K. Frank, 1939; Lewin, 1951). Achievement-related experience structures time almost more than anything else. Above all it is directed toward the future, fosters longer time spans, connects moments in time, and puts the succession of time periods in order. It also turns back to past incidents, as for instance, to affective states, resulting from success and failure which typically characterize the after-period of a course of action. The course of action itself shows a pronounced future time perspective (cf. below, Goal Structure, p. 67). Goal settings insofar as they are reality-oriented, are based on a putting together of past and future time perspectives (Lewin, 1951; Heckhausen & Roelofsen, 1962; cf. Chapter VIII). Increased socioeconomic status leads to a lengthening of time perspective, especially toward the future, which is characteristic for particular social classes (Leshan, 1952; Rosen, 1956; Douvan & Adelson, 1958).

The motivating characteristic of evaluative dispositions should phenomenologically be called more precisely an expectation from the viewpoint of time perspective. By this is meant the expectation that one will—or will not—carry a present state (actual state) over into a more satisfying end state as measured against certain standards of excellence (of the normative state). The experiencing of a discrepancy in terms of time between a present-existing and an anticipated-future situation is the real motivating force, phenomenologically speaking, that stimulates and directs perception and performance. Since the anticipation of a future situation, that is of success or failure, represents an expectation with positive or negative affects, and experiencing this expectation appears as either pleasant or unpleasant, or inviting or deterring, this results in either approach or avoidance behavior (cf. Heckhausen, 1963b; Fuchs, 1963). Because of the complex connection between time-perspective experiences and motivation, affective expectations should be given precedence in diagnosing motivation over the various dimensions of experience. These expectations represent important categories in all the scoring keys developed thus far for measuring motivation (e.g., goal anticipation). With respect to n Ach, not only the level of motivation must be connected with indicators of the span and structure of time perspective but also the direction in which the motive is oriented, that is, whether toward "Hope of Success" or "Fear of Failure."

This has been confirmed in a series of investigations employing quite different indicators. Ss with high n Ach make greater use of the future tense and dependent clauses, which indicates a contingent relation between present and future (Zatzkis, in McClelland *et al.*, 1953). They are better able to postpone gratification and when a choice is given between an immediate small reward and a future larger one, they frequently decide in favor of the larger [Mischel, 1961; Cameron & Storm, 1965; cf. Fisher, 1961; as well as the concept of the

"Arc of Expectation" (Spannungsbogen) in Künkel, 1928].
Low achievement disposition (inferred from the presence of
low school achievement) according to Davids and Sidman
(1962) and Strauss (1962) is accompanied by a greater sub-
jection to the present and by a lower ability to delay gratification. Highly motivated Ss[7] relate the experience of the person
depicted in the TAT to dates that lie further in the future and
give longer periods of total time perspective in general than
low-motivated Ss (Heckhausen, 1963b). The same applies
to the time structure of action (Ricks & Epley, cited in Mc-
Clelland, 1961). Good pupils display more anticipatory and
optimistic references to the future than poor ones in their
conversation as well as in fantasy stories, however, level of
intelligence and references to the future do not correlate
(Teahan, 1958). Foreseeable calculable risks in driving, which
might lead to traffic offenses and accidents, are handled better
by drivers with high achievement motivation (Hoyos, 1965).

The directionality of achievement motivation is no less
important than its strength. TAT stories of success-motivated
Ss contain longer ranges of future perspective than those of
failure-motivated Ss (Heckhausen, 1963b). In reproduction
from memory of time-related material [i.e., tasks that were
worked on yesterday with half of the results to be made
known tomorrow and the other half four weeks later (cf.
Ferdinand, 1959)], success-motivated Ss in contrast to failure-
motivated Ss remember more tasks to be reported on later and
fewer to be reported on sooner in time. Thus they are better
able to link successive stages in time perspective into one
unit (Götzl, 1960 in Heckhausen, 1963b). Based on questionnaire information (Vukovich et al., 1964), the success-motivated Ss, like the highly motivated Ss, prefer to keep their
"eyes on a big goal," and they prefer tasks that extend over

---

[7] Throughout this volume, this phrase means subjects who score
high on the total n Ach (or AM) score.

longer periods of time, need to be planned, and require decisions. They do not need success to occur soon; rather they are quite able to wait.

The successful businessman is characterized by a similar ability, that is, to recognize future possibilities and to adjust to them (McClelland, 1961). The risks involved in making a decision in advance can be balanced more realistically if the time perspective has a long range. The longer it is, the more distinct is the preference for a realistically calculated risk as has been shown by the moderate goal setting of highly motivated and success-motivated Ss (Heckhausen, 1963b). All these findings corroborate the relationships, discussed by Lewin (1953), among self-reliance, hope, perseverance ("morale"), and planning ahead for a better future. The close relationship between time perspective and various levels of reality in experience will be discussed in the next chapter.

Characteristic differences also appear in the qualitative perception of time as Knapp and Garbutt (1958, 1965) have shown in studies of preferences for poetic metaphors for time, grouped by factor analysis. Highly motivated Ss find their time experience best expressed in images indicating fast, directed movement, such as "a space ship in flight"; whereas less-motivated Ss express it in static images, such as "a quiet, motionless ocean." Heckhausen (1963b) found similar clusters of factors with German subjects and confirmed the connection with the strength of achievement motivation. An analysis of the "dynamic fast-moving" images preferred by the highly motivated Ss proved to be remarkably informative about the outlook of people with predominant success or failure expectations. Success-motivated Ss look upon time as a goal-directed, fast movement; whereas failure-motivated Ss see in it an aimless, incessant stream of motion. The former seem to let themselves be carried confidently by time and hurry forward; they use it for planned, straight-forward motion; the latter, however, seem to consider themselves fatefully abandoned to a whirling, driving time.

Knapp has found further differences in experience and perception of time in a series of investigations. As a motivational measure he used preferences of highly motivated Ss for subdued colors (blue and green tartans preferred over red and yellow, 1958). Time spans extending equally into the past and future seem to be closer to the present for the highly motivated Ss; thus the entire time range is more compressed. For them, events in more recent history extend less far back into the past, and the end of a current event is expected earlier than it will actually occur (Green & Knapp, 1959). There are also characteristic differences in the attitude toward the lapse of time in everyday life. Highly motivated Ss become angry if the clock is not exact; they are worried when they do not know the time; they have a bad conscience if they sleep late in the morning or otherwise waste time (Knapp, 1962; cf. Argyle & Robinson, 1962). Highly motivated Ss are able to judge more correctly the time taken by a piece of music, which is underestimated by Ss with low n Ach. This is probably because the latter are more absorbed by the music they are listening to (Knapp & Green, 1961). Highly motivated Ss reproduce acoustically presented time spans with faster hand motions (duPreez, 1964).

III. LEVELS OF REALITY

An achievement-related experience is often characterized by certain peculiarities in relation to reality. It is able to encompass different levels of reality at the same time and to move among them. Up to now very different things have been included under the headings of "reality" and "unreality" (cf. Metzger, 1954, as to various kinds of "reality"). This distinction should not be equated with the distinction between "personally important" and "unimportant," as it was by J. F. Brown (1933) because he found that both were linked to differential recall of tasks previously performed. His result was an artifact due to a Zeigarnik effect induced by the testing technique, as Ferdinand has shown (1959). It is equally doubtful whether something further ahead in the future is more unreal just because of its distance away in terms of time perspective. The poorer recall that Ferdinand found associated with "time perspective distance" (not confirmed by Götzl, 1960) does not need to be explained in terms of the higher "degree of fluidity" of psychic systems in the plane of unreality (Lewin, 1935), but rather can be explained sufficiently by a lower level of salience, i.e., by differences in contextual support. Besides, something personally important may be quite unreal and something unimportant may be real.

Frequently, different levels of psychic reality are said to apply to different modes of behavior. Thus, acting is said to be more real than speaking, and speaking in turn more real than thinking. Actually, each of these modes may show widely varying levels of reality. The manner in which an achievement goal is "made real" depends on the nature of the task (Mahler, 1933). In the case of problem solving, action is usually inappropriate and cannot be substituted for the thinking which makes a solution possible. The differences between serious and playful activity also do not coincide with the difference between reality and unreality (Sliosberg, 1934). Play is an area of life, separate from the reality of everyday person-environment relationships. It has its own definitions of meaning, in which the proceedings are quite real or, better still, "quasi real" (Heckhausen, 1964b), but not unreal.

It is possible to define levels of reality in terms of the various transitory stages that exist between something actual and something just imagined, desired, or feared. Future time perspective includes levels which extend from the possible to the absolutely impossible, from the certain to the uncertain. Levels of past time perspective range from something that has actually happened to what could or should have happened. Since Freud (1900, 1908), great importance has been attached to unreal behavior. Thus, wishful fantasies as in daydreaming are said to provide a substitute satisfaction for those needs which are denied satisfaction in reality.

That fantasy behavior appears to have a compensatory or substitute function has been established only in isolated cases even for such tabooed motives as sexuality and aggression (e.g., Feshbach, 1955). Perhaps it is necessary to postulate some kind of cathartic effect for "unreal behavior" but its governing conditions have not yet been clarified (cf. Feshbach, 1961; Berkowitz & Rawlings, 1963). Frequently the diminution of manifest impulses after expression of a thought in the plane of unreality is less a cathartic effect than a consequence of reality-oriented inhibition caused by expression of the thought (Epstein, 1962). On the other hand, fantasy can, under certain conditions, actually intensify the tendency to carry out tabooed behavior, as in the passive, empathic experience of a spectator (Berkowitz, 1964; also Weiner, 1966).

As to achievement motivation, the substitute value is probably small of wish fulfillments that anticipate the overcoming of difficulties, or even reaching the goal. Unreal "substitute" actions do not lead to relaxation in the pursuit of a real achievement goal (Mahler, 1933). They are perceived as increasingly inappropriate the stronger the arousal of motivation (Sliosberg, 1934). On the other hand, unrealistic attempts at problem-solving may occur if the goal cannot be reached despite all efforts and if one cannot "go out of the field" (Dembo, 1931).

It would be strange if achievement-related fantasy behavior had a substitute value of great importance. For if it did, it would result in chronic failure because reality is not altered even by intense wishful fantasies or by substitute actions in fantasy; and chronic failure would in the long run result in heavy social sanctions. Occasionally in special pathological cases the conditions of reality may foster development of unreal normative states, through the failure of the reality checking process. It is questionable, however, if one can still speak of achievement motivation in connection with unreal evaluative dispositions which forego any contact with reality. Men who answer on a questionnaire that they have a preference for achievement-related wish fantasies have low motivation (AM) according to Vukovich *et al.* (1964) and high test anxiety (TAQ); the same is true for women according to Reiter (1963). On the other hand, Singer and Schonbar (1961) found that women who abandon themselves frequently to a daydreamlike inner life produce quite a number of achievement themes in reported daydreams and original stories, including themes of effortless gain of property and esteem.

It is another matter when a person chooses easier or different goals as *substitutes* because he has failed or because he perceives certain tasks as too difficult. In many such cases it is not a question of real substitution but rather the selection of a new goal while the old one is given up temporarily or forever. Even when they do represent a substitution, the new goals are not strictly speaking "unreal." Even success achieved by chance which is not perceived as a personal accomplishment does not have to be experienced as "unreal" as Hoppe (1930) points out. Chance, good luck, and bad luck are perceived as uncharacteristic of achievement situations, but not as unreal. Besides, even critical adults tend to underestimate chance factors in an accomplishment in order to credit it to their own competence; on the other hand, they blame adverse circumstances or chance for failures for which they are personally responsible (Hoppe, 1930; Heckhausen, 1955; Mehl, 1962). In both cases, it is a question not of different levels of reality of experience but of deceptions and self-deceptions ("rationalizations") about what is actually taking place (see below p. 62). Finally, TAT stories do not have to be considered "unreal" behavior designed to provide substitute satisfaction merely because they are fantasy formations as Lazarus and his collaborators argue (1961; Vogel *et al.*, 1958, 1959). On the contrary, under suitable conditions, TAT stories contain expressions of achievement-related evaluative dispositions that correspond to psychic reality, as their relationships to numerous behavioral criteria demonstrate.

In the course of action an occasional "unreal" performance experience is the rule rather than the exception. Thus, the goal aspired to is anticipated as already reached in imagination, especially when difficulties arise and interruptions and postponements become necessary. This is "unreal" but it is not a substitute for actual realization of the goal in the sense that it results in a relaxation of efforts to achieve. As a pause to look into the future, it motivates and can intensify the push toward the goal and stimulate effort. After the conclusion of an achievement test, unreal experience in the form of daydreaming increases anxiety about failure (Singer & Rowe, 1962).

As a rule, two levels of reality accompany experiences occurring in time. Structured on the top of reality — as a past event, the present situation, or a future event considered real — is an area of unreality consisting of thoughts like "Oh, if I had," "Should," "Would," etc. Feelings of hope and fear, relief and disappointment (cf. Mowrer, 1960; Feather, 1963c) are basic types in a three-dimensional frame of reference built out of time elapsed, time in prospect, and level of reality. Thus, for instance, disappointment is the becoming unreal (level of reality) of an expectation (time in prospect) formerly (elapsed time) considered real. The feeling of remorse ("Oh, if I only had") can be considered as a discrepancy in the past between reality ("it was") and unreality ("it should have been").

It is the nature of future perspective to be unreality-oriented to a special degree. Thus, goal settings may in particular display high levels of unreality, as the research on level of aspiration has shown. The level of unreality does not have a simple relationship to strength of motivation. It neither grows with motive strength nor with either of the motivational tendencies toward success and failure (HS and FF). It is noteworthy that expectation of success leads to a greater *reality* in goal setting than fear of failure (as judged objectively by hindsight). Success-motivated Ss make greater allowance for what they consider to be actually attainable than do failure-motivated Ss, who either stay cautiously below the actually attainable or go speculatively above it (Heckhausen, 1963b; Meyer *et al.*, 1965).

Developmentally speaking it is possible to establish the ontogenetic primacy of unreality in achievement-oriented experience as it relates to the past and the future. This unreality has to yield, even in early childhood, to the increasing pressure of reality, of what actually happens (Heckhausen & Roelofsen, 1962). Once desired events have begun to correspond to actual or probable occurrences, there arises during the fourth year the possibility of conflict after failure between reality and unreality in viewing the past ("as it was and as it should have been"), and if prospects of failure predominate this is also true for future perspective ("as it probably will be and as it is wanted to be"). If success and failure outcomes are equally probable, children are unable to experience this conflict until about a year later, from about the age of 4½ on. About this time, it is possible to observe the first goal settings in the sense of level of aspiration (Heckhausen & Wagner, 1965).

It should be noted that the experienced degree of reality of something should not be confused with its objective reality. No matter how closely these two may be related, and no matter how much the subjective probability of the occurrence of an event may approach the objective probability, the highly significant problem remains of determining how experience and action are tied to reality. With regard to achievement orientation, it is above all a question of the extent to which the experienced degree of difficulty of a task corresponds to the actual degree of difficulty, or the extent to which the subjective probabilities of success and failure correspond to the objective probabilities. Cohen and Hansel (1955) found that high objective degrees of difficulty are underestimated and low ones overestimated, and that most exact prediction occurs when the objective probability of success is around 30%; according to Howard (1963), the figure is around 45% (cf. Feather, 1963a; also Schmidt & Zarn, 1964). Individual differences are characteristic. Thus, success-motivated Ss in comparison with failure-motivated Ss overestimate the probability of success, as Brody (1963, with n Ach) and Feather (1963a, with the use of AAT but not with n Ach) found. They tend to estimate their chances of success as higher than "fear of failure" Ss do on an upcoming task of moderate difficulty (Feather, 1965a, with the combined measures of n Ach and MAS). Evidently if success motivation predominates, the prospects of success rather than of failure (which are mathematically but not psychologically complementary) are kept in mind so that the probability of failure is less salient (Heckhausen, 1963b; cf. below, Level of Aspiration, p. 100).

Finally, the subjective probability of success also appears to grow with increasing goal incentive values especially in the middle range of objective probabilities. This, however, has not as yet been proved for the prediction of events depending on achievement[8] although it has been proved for events depending on chance and involving different reward values

---

[8] Diggory and Morlock (1964), however, found a reverse relationship for an activity depending on achievement. This is only an apparently contradictory finding, though, since it was obtained under very special and mainly failure-inducing conditions (cf. below, p. 90).

(Crandall, Solomon, & Kellaway, 1955; Jessor & Readio, 1957). Yet up to the present, these questions have only been treated within the framework of the so-called theories of decision (cf. W. Edwards, 1954; Feather 1959b) that are concerned with consumer attitudes and risk preferences with respect to uncertain events with varying reward values (cf. Feather, 1959a; Cohen & Hansel, 1961; Mehl, 1962).

CHAPTER V

CONFLICT

Conflict-proneness is a sign of the presence of achievement motivation. It is kindled by the occurrence of failure. Thus, the experience of failure-motivated Ss is more conflict-laden. The conflict is typically of the approach-avoidance type (cf. Lewin, 1935, p. 89 ff.). This is more difficult to resolve than other forms of conflict because the tendencies to approach and avoid are related to the same thing, namely, the achievement goal. Achievement-related conflicts can be separated into two basic types on the basis of the time involved. The first is characterized by future perspective, is directed toward a goal, and is formed around *expectation* of failure. The second is characterized by past perspective and is linked to a past failure. It is formed around the *experience* of failure.

I. EXPECTATION OF FAILURE

Conflicts of this kind appear in connection with goal setting. The incentive value of a goal increases with the difficulty involved and this in turn increases the probability of failure (cf. Lewin, Dembo, Festinger, & Sears, 1944; Feather, 1959a, 1959b). The uncertainty about the outcome is greatest in the area of medium difficulty since experienced probabilities of success and failure counterbalance each other. The more the approach and avoidance tendencies (Hope of Success and

53

Fear of Failure) balance each other out, the greater may be the conflict; the intensity of this conflict depends also on the absolute strength of the two tendencies. It follows that goals with equal prospects of success and failure ought to be avoided most if a person is trying to avoid conflict. As we shall see, this is true for failure-motivated but not for success-motivated persons. Do the latter tolerate or even prefer conflict? Probably conflict does not have much significance for them because they are not as much disturbed by a 50% probability of failure as are the failure-motivated persons. The latter resolve their conflicts not only by cautiously setting low goals but, paradoxically, also by overly high goal setting. High goal setting is evidently intended to intensify one's efforts in order to overcome the failure-avoidant tendencies and thus to diminish the resultant conflict. (See for more details Chapter VIII.)

Thus, goal settings are frequently linked to approach-avoidance conflicts. If there is a choice of several goal alternatives having similar degrees of difficulty, a multiple approach-avoidance conflict may result (e.g., in the selection of a career) which will be difficult to resolve. If goal setting occurs in a social situation, the approach-avoidance conflict may be expressed in the so-called "splitting" of the level of aspiration (Heckhausen, 1955). A goal that can be reached with certainty is announced while a higher one is secretly aimed for.

A further characteristic of conflict is rigid goal setting. Failure-motivated persons burdened with conflict are less ready to take into account their actual level of achievement with its implied prospects of success. They avoid the renewed arousal of conflict by keeping to a goal setting which has in the meantime become obsolete (Heckhausen, 1963b). Cohen and Zimbardo (1962) found that something similar was involved in cases of great, situationally produced conflict. Persons who, after many vain attempts to solve a task, can be induced to risk further failure voluntarily in additional trials, do not lower the level of aspiration below the point at which they have failed. On the other hand, if the experience of failure is less pronounced and the discrepancy between the desire to solve the task and the fear of failure is consequently smaller, the readiness to lower the level of aspiration is greater. This finding has been explained by Cohen and Zimbardo in terms of the Theory of Cognitive Dissonance (Festinger, 1957). In the first case there is a greater dissonance between fear of failure and the resolution to continue to face failure. More intense conflict is avoided by a weakening in failure avoidance motivation that is supposed to be achieved by maintaining the obsolete level of aspiration. This interpretation is plausible but not conclusive.

Symptoms of conflict occur outside the area of goal setting. A person carefully takes precautions to preclude failure. The accent here is on assuring success or avoiding failure. It is amazing how resourceful even small children are in the resolution of conflict by taking precautions (Heckhausen & Roelofsen, 1962). Thus, for instance, in a competition, the rules of the game are suddenly redefined to the disadvantage of a rival.

Conflict-prone expectations of failure also lead to less appropriate solution attempts and, if the situation permits it, to interruptions in solving a task. Conflict promotes evasions and "going out of the field." This may be the reason why failure-motivated students turn their home work in later than their success-motivated fellow students (Heckhausen, 1963b). Persistence in solving a difficult problem also depends on conflict. Feather (1961; 1963b) found that failure-motivated Ss abandon their efforts toward a solution sooner than success-motivated Ss if the problem is described as easy (low probability of failure). Since the problem, however, was actually unsolvable it was experienced as increasingly difficult in the course of the fruitless efforts to solve it and thus it soon entered the area of medium difficulty (50% probability of failure) which, as mentioned above, intensifies the conflict experienced by failure-motivated persons. On the other hand, if the task is described as difficult from the beginning, then failure-motivated persons persevere *more* in fruitless efforts to find a solution! Evidently this is because they do not have to go through the stage of conflict involved in working on a problem of medium difficulty (cf. Smith, 1964). Thinking about the way to solve problems may be impaired by conflict experiences. Failure-motivated persons under time pressure solve fewer problems than success-motivated persons (Bartmann, 1963). Time pressure evidently accentuates expectation of failure to such an extent that the failure-motivated S enters into a critical stage of conflict. Ryan and Lakie (1965) found analogous results with a perceptual motor task given under neutral versus competitive conditions (cf. p. 76).

According to Miller's (1944, 1959) conflict model one would expect that as the goal approaches, failure expectation rises more rapidly than success expectation, and a point will be reached in the course of approach—at a given psychic distance before the goal—at which failure expectation becomes stronger than expectation of success. The balance in the ratio of strengths of the two tendencies at this point in the course of a solution attempt leads to an intensification of conflict that may result in a termination of the problem-solving efforts (as in Feather, 1961, 1963b). According to the same model, the distance between the point of intersection of the two gradients and the goal depends not only on their different slopes but also on differences in the level above the baseline of the two gradients. Bartmann's previously mentioned finding could be explained by a change in the level of one gradient. Time pressure could have increased the failure expectation of the failure-motivated Ss to such a degree that a stage of acute conflict was created at the beginning of the problem-solving efforts, i.e., at a great distance from the goal.

Findings by Scott (1956) could be understood in the same way. He obtained stories written under relaxed and extremely tense conditions. In the latter instance, students were told that the test results would be used to determine which participants would be selected for an oversubscribed course. With induced ego involvement, not all Ss showed an increase in n Ach scores as is generally the case. A minority, the so-called avoiders, in fact showed *reduced n* Ach values! Their stories are shorter, show less realistic treatment of achievement-related content of the pictures, contain fewer activities directed toward a solution, and more resignation in the face of emerging difficulties, and, finally, more rarely lead to a successful outcome. The expectation of failure of the avoiders has evidently been increased to such an extent under these arousal conditions that they arrive at a stage of acute conflict. In control tests without threatening arousal, their stories did not differ from those of others whose stories, written under conditions of ego involvement, did not contain any of the symptoms of conflict mentioned. (Compare paradoxical effects of arousal, p. 11 above; for instance Meyer *et al.*, 1965).

Ertel (1964) has shown with a factor analytic typology based on the semantic differential that the mere announcement of an intelligence test arouses conflict in students as long as their normative achievement motivation is failure-oriented rather than success-oriented. The ratings of the impending intelligence test show characteristic similarity in both motivation groups with two independently established reference profiles which concern tasks of "great difficulty" where in one case "one hopes nevertheless to achieve success in the end," and in the other case "one is afraid of not achieving success despite the efforts made." Success motivation (HS-FF of AM) correlates positively with the similarity between the reference profile of the first type of task (where it is confidently hoped to overcome the difficulty) and the characteristic profile based on the valence of the impending intelligence test; success motivation correlates negatively with the similarity between the profile of the second type of task (which evokes more acute experience of conflict between expectation of failure and efforts to solve the task) and the characteristic profile of the intelligence test. The findings cited show that conflicts with a future time perspective are not only dependent on the situation but also on normative motivation. In this connection, failure-motivated persons exhibit more potential for conflict ("fear of not achieving success") than do success-motivated persons, as is to be expected.

II. RISK-TAKING

The extent to which conflicts with varying degrees of time perspective are approached rather than avoided ought to be influenced by individual differences in risk-taking. Since David Katz (1953) introduced the concept of the margin of safety (Sicherheitsmarginal) as the size of the margin of safety which an individual prefers to employ, there has been no lack of attempts to isolate this personality variable. However, the results have been disappointing. Hardly any agreement has been obtained among measures based on questionnaires and behavioral experiments involving assigned task performances that can be achieved safely or not depending on the amount of time, care, or effort at precision expended (Slovic, 1962).

Before concluding from the above that risk-taking is not a personality variable, we must see whether something else can be isolated with these methods, for instance, the different value weight people attach to various tasks or to items in a questionnaire, since it can be assumed that something of more importance will result in a greater margin of safety than something deemed to be of no consequence. The influence of such differences in evaluation seems to be involved when

Merz, Weber, and Wieja (1963) discovered higher correlations among margin of safety test variables after having dichotomized Ss into a group of success-motivated persons and another group of failure-motivated persons. Differences in skill and ability in various areas of activity should also be taken into consideration. An instrument for testing risk-taking properly speaking has apparently not yet been found. Such an instrument ought to obtain the degree of risk which one is ready to enter into *for its own sake*. Lifelike test situations naturally have narrow limits since Ss cannot be exposed to real dangers that might result in the loss of property, reputation, or health.

It is more expedient to obtain groups of people after they have experienced incidents with dangerous results. Drivers with different frequencies of accidents and violations have been examined by Hoyos (1965) as to their achievement motivation and driving habits. Highly motivated Ss prove themselves by taking calculated risks which result in violations *outside* the area of driving itself (e.g., overloading, driving without license, parking violations). As to driving itself, persons preferring overly high risks and those who prefer subnormal risks, are less often guilty of a traffic violation or an accident, the higher their achievement motivation. Failure-motivated persons observe traffic laws more conscientiously, and success-motivated persons do so only if they deem them reasonable and advisable. All in all, the notion Hoyos has developed of viewing driving as an achievement-related process with various kinds and degrees of risk seems to be promising for psychological insight into achievement behavior (cf. Hoyos, 1963).

Although risk-taking and level of aspiration do have a certain similarity they are not the same thing. It is risky to take an exam without preparation, but this does not indicate a high level of aspiration. On the other hand, the two concepts may legitimately be used interchangeably when a person has to decide about something, or set a level of aspiration, when the outcome has an appreciable element of chance in it. The tendency to use the two terms synonymously in the United States (cf. Atkinson, 1957; McClelland, 1958b) has been promoted by the interest in research concerning the relation between entrepreneurial behavior and economic growth on the one hand (cf. McClelland, 1961), and between consumer buying habits and attitudes toward competition and games of chance on the other hand (W. Edwards, 1954; Feather, 1959a, 1959b; Scodel, Ratoosh, & Minas, 1959). High achievement motivation (*n* Achievement) is linked to the taking of moderate, "calculated" risks as well as to an aversion for daring speculations that result in winnings by chance only under favorable circumstances but which usually lead to the early ruin of an enterprise (McClelland, 1961; cf. below, pp. 94 f.).

Risk-taking in betting and games of chance is not of an achievement-related nature since the end result is not influenced by one's own ability. Such an observation presupposes the ability to differentiate between chance and achievement-related success and failure. According to Mehl (1962) this ability does not exist before the age of about 10. Feather (1959a) did not find even in 12-year-old children a difference between achievement-related and chance tasks so far as preferences for various probabilities of success were concerned. In poker and dice games with varying chances of winning and stakes of real, albeit small, amounts of money, Littig (1959, 1963b) found that highly motivated *Ss* (*n* Achievement) prefer the least risks and not moderately high risks (as is the case with setting levels of aspiration for achievement activities). Thus their risk-taking in games of chance is minimal. This has been confirmed by Hancock and Teevan (1964) and by Raynor and Smith (1965; see below p. 95). Although Atkinson, Bastian, Earl, and Litwin (1960) have noticed a certain tendency in highly motivated *Ss* to prefer degrees of moderate risk while betting in imaginary games of chance, the existence of a transfer effect can not be precluded since games of skill were included in the experiments.

Mehl (1962) offered students the choice of receiving either a gift of 100 Marks or of drawing lots, one of which would yield a prize of 20 Marks and the other of 500 Marks. Those who take their chances in drawing lots in preference to a certain 100 Marks and thus risk losing a small prize for the sake of a larger one are also more inclined to blame failures in achievement situations on chance. Risk-taking in lotteries and games of chance, therefore, does not go hand in hand with an objective and self-critical attitude in achievement-related situations. Wendt (1961) has traced the conditions for development of risk-taking in earliest childhood. The relative predictability of the mother's behavior during the sensitive phases of prelanguage development seems to have an "imprinting" effect on the child.

III. RESOLUTION OF CONFLICT AFTER FAILURE

Failure is followed by an experience of conflict in past time perspective. The conflict expresses itself in various attempts at resolution. Attempts to classify reactions to conflict are sparse. McClelland and Apicella (1945) have made the most thorough attempt using scattered findings of other investigators as well as the verbal reactions to frustration obtained in their own investigations. They differentiate between goal-oriented and defense-oriented reactions—a distinction that coincides with our classification of conflicts into those with future time perspective and those with past time perspective. Helm (1954) and Heckhausen (1955) have reported on various forms of defensive reactions to conflict. Let us now review our findings for 3- to 6-year-old children (Heckhausen & Roelofsen, 1962) who show a variety of reactions to failure that adults could hardly surpass. The children experienced failure in competing in a social situation as is the rule for achievement-related transactions. The typical forms of expressive behavior after success and failure, as well as the attitudes toward conflict, have been documented in a movie (Heckhausen, Ertel, & Kiekheben-Roelofsen, 1964).

First there is a large group of reactions signifying *denial* of the outcome. The experienced failure is denied (with discernible "bad conscience"), undone, excused, or glossed over. Glossing over or "rationalization" may be a highly developed defense in some adults (Heckhausen, 1955). Mehl (1962) found further that adolescents have a tendency to attribute success to one's own ability, and failure to chance. This can still be observed in adults (students) in a diminished form.

A second group of reactions consists of *withdrawal,* going out of the field in numerous ways, beginning with psychological flight from the achievement situation through interruption in favor of interpolated activities, and ending with the subtle restructuring of the task. Aggressive behavior, too, may appear occasionally if the situation permits this, and if there is no prospect of consequences that would produce anxiety. Dembo (1931) was able to record, under conditions of prolonged frustration, a growing "underlying affective tension," outbursts of anger and even violence (in adults!) directed at the experimenter. Aggressive responses are, as a rule, of a verbal nature, directed more or less covertly at the experimenter, or even directed openly at the self (McClelland & Apicella, 1945). Conflict seems to become less acute through expressing psychic tension and, in extreme cases, through the destruction of an apparently hopeless situation.

A further group of reactions consists of a variety of *substitute activities.* They form various stages, ranging from substitute satisfaction in unrelated areas of activities, through compensations in related areas, to goal shifting within the same task. The substitute value is greater the more similar the substitute activities are to the tasks failed (Mahler, 1933). As mentioned before, unreal substitute activities contribute little to the resolution of an achievement-related conflict. Nevertheless it is possible that even adults have recourse to substitute activities in cases of prolonged frustration which they cannot escape ("practicing magic," Dembo, 1931).

Weiner appears to have demonstrated (1965a) that interpolated success experiences on a task involving skill, i.e., on a task with some substitute value, can lessen the effects of a conflict based on past failure. Thereafter more conflict-ridden individuals (low n Ach) will resume interrupted tasks than relatively nonconflicted individuals (high n Ach). This can be explained in terms of N. E. Miller's conflict model (1944). Success experiences lower the avoidance gradient for failure-motivated Ss, lessen their conflict, and result in a net increase in approach responses.

A mature, i.e., adequate, form of conflict resolution is to *make good* or *erase* the failure by increased or renewed efforts in the pursuit of the same task. Time-perspective faces in two directions (as is the case of many substitute activities); on the one hand it is directed toward past failure which has to be overcome, and on the other hand it is directed ahead toward the achievement goal which has to be attained. Highly motivated (success-oriented) persons decide on the future orientation when choosing between tasks which they have either solved already or were not able to solve (Coopersmith, 1960). Such "making good" appears increasingly often between the age of 2 and 6 while resolution of conflict through denial and withdrawal become rarer. However, the frequency of substitute activities does not appear to be dependent on age (Heckhausen & Roelofsen, 1962). According to Mahler (1933), substitute completions of unfinished activities have as much substitute value for adults as they have for children. In contrast to denial and withdrawal, substitute activities represent an appropriate way in which to resolve failure.

They pile up after attempts not to accept failure. Furthermore, the various attempts at conflict resolution do not correlate; they seem to possess qualities of uniqueness and individual specificity. "Making good" alone seems to preclude
withdrawal, which simply underlines the fact that these two
forms of conflict resolution are functionally opposed. In this
respect it seems that even small children show a disposition
to prefer either a more goal-oriented or defense-oriented
method of resolving conflicts — a preference which results in a
strengthening of success-approaching or failure-avoiding
motivational tendencies (cf. Heckhausen & Wagner, 1965).

IV. CONFLICTS WITH OTHER MOTIVES

Up to the present, conflicts with other motives of the
approach-avoidant type have hardly been investigated.
Sampson (1963) has established such a conflict by requiring
that female students who want to learn syllables quickly
according to instructions will have to carry out an unpleasant
activity when they finish, i.e., those reaching the goal quickly
use the time remaining to shock some white mice. It is
apparent that the connection between achievement motivation and performing well on the learning task is lost under
such conditions. Investigations concerned with conflict of
the approach-approach type have been carried out more frequently. French (1956) put achievement motivation in conflict with need for affiliation. She asked her subjects to choose
one of two partners for a task: either a liked person who,
however, was known to have little ability for this task, or
someone who had proved successful at the task but whom they
disliked. Ss with high achievement motivation and low need
for affiliation (according to FTI) solved the conflict according
to expectation: they chose as a partner the disliked but capable person. For such people the successful solution of the

task is dominant and the social situation is subordinate (cf. Rosenfeld, 1964). Persons with high need for affiliation and low achievement motivation made a reverse decision.

Something similar is reported by Walker and Heyns (1962). In an ingenious test arrangement they put pairs of male students or of female students into a kind of competition with one another. One member of the pair had to code a text which the other ostensibly had to decode immediately afterward. When this partner protested in a (feigned) written note that he could not keep up with the work and that the other should slow down the coding, most of the women but very few men complied. In this case, too, differences in the salience of the two motives become important. Thus, those women who were more achievement-motivated than affiliation-motivated decided on continuing the work without delay. Of the Ss with equally strong salience of both motives, i.e., with maximized conflict, one-half kept up their work tempo and one-half decreased it.

These experiments can also be considered from the viewpoint of the effect of pressure for conformity by a social group. After it had been shown that highly motivated persons yield less to such pressure (McClelland et al., 1953, p. 286; Krebs, 1958), attempts were made to investigate conflicts between achievement motivation and strivings for conformity. Samelson (1958) has found that the connections are more complex than had first been assumed. Thus, highly motivated persons may conform more than persons of lesser motivation under certain conflicting circumstances when the majority opinion seems to constitute a standard of excellence for the achievement in question. Above all, significant contrasting effects of achievement motivation and need for affiliation have been demonstrated (cf. Hardy, 1957; Groesbeck, 1958; Mischel, 1961).

CHAPTER VI

THE GENERAL STRUCTURE OF GOALS AND PERFORMANCE

Achievement motivation is directed toward certain end results that are produced by one's own ability: namely, to achieve success and to avoid failure. Achievement motivation, therefore, is markedly goal-directed. It pushes a person toward the "natural" outcome of a linked series of acts. This necessitates a strictly ordered serial occurrence of these acts. However, there are special forms of activity that do not relate systematically to a final goal in this way. Achievement-related activities are occasionally engaged in for their own sake only and not for the purpose of concluding the activity by reaching a goal, nor for any other extrinsic purpose. This may be the case, for instance, in problem-solving (as in crossword puzzles, chess) or in practicing certain skills (e.g., handicrafts). The fluctuating vicissitudes of the problem-solving process are experienced as pleasant, even as titillating. Reaching the goal and success too early may be regretted (Henle, 1956). This kind of achievement-related goal structuring, like play, falls into the category of "purposeless activities" (cf. Berlyne, 1960; Heckhausen, 1964b).

A continuous overview of the goal is characteristic for achievement motivation. We have already discussed the phenomenal aspects of expectation and time perspective. If one looks at the course of action, the importance of a continuous overview in time becomes obvious since a chain of actions may be interrupted by periods of hours, nights, weeks, or months, if not years. Another characteristic of achievement motivation is the constant return to an interrupted task, to something previously abandoned, and the resumption of the main thread of action. Thus a complex and long-lasting structure of main, side, and subactivities is created which leads through an orderly series of subgoals to the main goal proper, be it ever so distant. Planning becomes necessary in order to order the succession and functional arrangement of the chain of actions. This overlapping time-structuring of activities, which H. A. Murray (1951) called "serial," is what distinguishes achievement motivation from many other motives. A large section of the research findings can be discussed in terms of the phases which follow each other in an achievement-related performance. We will be guided by this phase sequence in the following chapters.

CHAPTER VII

FOREPERIOD:
VALENCE AND MOTIVE AROUSAL

The foreperiod includes transactions that precede perform-ance and determine its direction, strategy, intensity, dura-tion, etc. What is involved is an actualization of motive potential or motive arousal. Motivation may also be described in terms of its correlate in the external world: the valence of the situation. Although in a phenomenological sense valence appears as an independent characteristic of the situation, functionally it does have a close connection to the motivational state. The normative level of motivation deter-mines the frame of reference in terms of which valences are formed and changed. In order to stress this relationship be-tween person and situation we have used the concept of apperception (thematization) in the discussion of evaluative dispositions. It is synonymous with the concept of valence but it places greater emphasis on the extent to which the ex-perience of the situation depends on motivation. As an aspect of achievement motivation, it is important to delineate the nature and extent of situations which are apperceived as achievement-related (or, in other words, which have an achievement-related valence). In this connection, we shall again discuss a few issues using the theory of motivation based on gradients of expectation (Heckhausen, 1963a; Fuchs, 1963). An expectation gradient has several determi-nants. One portion determines the discrepancy (as judged) between a present and a future state; another portion determines the psychic distance between a present and a future state which is anticipated as the end point in the action sequence.

I. DISCREPANCY BETWEEN A PRESENT AND A FUTURE STATE

It would be possible to obtain the discrepancy (the "difference in level") between the beginning and end of an expectation gradient if it were feasible to fix the experience of the present and of the future state. Experimental attempts have been made to vary discrepancies by introducing incentives in the form of a tempting goal or a threatening event (varying the future state). It is also possible to make the present state unsatisfactory or insecure. Finally, it is possible to do both in order to make both the present and the future state personally important (ego-involving). The possibilities are numerous. Chapters could be filled if one were to enumerate the attempts that have been made thus far to arouse motivation (e.g., by "ego involvement"). Thus, fantasy productions have shown again and again that achievement-related content increases if discrepancies of the kind described above (between present and future states) are created by instructions or pretest conditions (cf. McClelland *et al.*, 1953; French, 1955b; Haber & Alpert, 1958; Hayashi & Habu, 1962b, and many others; rare exceptions are: Vogel *et al.*, 1958; Peak, 1960). Success themes in TAT stories decrease greatly and failure themes increase markedly after a failure-inducing achievement test (Meyer *et al.*, 1965, using AM).

Much variance appears in the results obtained with these crude methods. Martire (1956), for instance, found that Ss with a large discrepancy between achievement-oriented real self and ideal self even under relaxed conditions produced as many achievement-related fantasies as other persons did under stronger arousal conditions (cf. similar findings by Coopersmith, 1959, and Reimanis, 1964). Scott (1956) found a group of persons who produced more achievement fantasies under relaxed than under aroused conditions (that is, when arousal consisted in announcing that some participants in an oversubscribed course would have to be eliminated on the basis of this test).

Such variations of production of achievement-related themes in fantasy can be elucidated further if one takes into account not only the present and future states of being as the E tries to define them for the Ss, but also the normative motivational states that determine the meaning of concrete experimental variations in procedure. Thus, Martire's exceptional group of Ss was highly motivated, and for such a group strong achievement motivation is aroused by even small discrepancies between what is and what should be. Scott's exceptional group, however, was failure-motivated; large discrepancies (prospect of a threatening future state) caused them to avoid achievement-related themes in their fantasy productions. The size of the discrepancy in the gradient of expectation can be determined more exactly if normative motivational level is taken into consideration as a frame of reference for defining varying states. It can be ascertained relatively easily with the aid of the TAT method. Since the TAT gives expression of a sort to "what should be," it can be taken as a rough approximation of the expected future state so that in order to determine the discrepancy one needs to know only the value the person places on the present state which (again as a rough substitute simplification in lieu of a better method) might be set for all Ss via a definition of the "objectively" existing situation (cf. Heckhausen, 1963a, see footnote p. 623).

We do not intend to pursue the problem any further from the methodological viewpoint. No attempt has yet been made to employ the construct of "Discrepancy in the Gradient of Expectation." Besides, it is evident that the achievement-related apperception or valence of a situation is a function not only of normative motivation but also of the discrepancy between a present and a future state. If the discrepancy is lacking or not sufficiently salient (especially in comparison with other frames of reference), even the strongest potential motivation cannot be actualized. Motive arousal does not take place.

This has been shown in a series of investigations. In an experiment involving tachistoscopic thresholds, highly motivated Ss recognized achievement-related words sooner than Ss with lower motivation only if the task has been previously related to achievement (Moulton, Raphelson, Kristofferson, & Atkinson, 1958). In a pure game of chance, highly motivated Ss do not react in an achievement-related way: they prefer the least possible risk instead of a moderate risk as in achievement tasks (Littig, 1959, 1963b; Hancock & Teevan, 1964; Raynor & Smith, 1965). The correlation between achievement motivation and performance is also modified by the "demand character" or valence of the situation. The correlation diminishes when arousal is no longer solely of an achievement-related nature, e.g., when monetary rewards are involved, and when a desire is induced to comply with the wishes of E. Atkinson and Reitman (1956) have obtained such findings with respect to both the quality and quantity of mental arithmetic problems solved (after Düker, 1949). Atkinson (1958a) found a relation between achievement motivation and arithmetic achievement only when a small reward ($1.25) was involved but not with a larger reward ($2.50).

If the E appeals more strongly for cooperation from his Ss, performance no longer correlates with achievement motivation but rather with need for affiliation, as Atkinson and Raphelson have established (1956) with a sensorimotor speed task, and French (1955b) with a coding task. Reitman (1960), however, has tried in vain to verify this findings. In agreement with the previously mentioned authors, Vogel *et al.* (1959) have shown that the highest motive activation occurs when situational arousal corresponds in content to the dominant potential motivation (in this case differentiated by questionnaires used with extreme groups and not by the TAT method). Highly motivated *S*s do not apperceive the situation as less achievement-related if they work for the group rather than for themselves (French, 1958b). Need for affiliation, on the other hand, correlates with performance only when working for the group is involved. However, if a stimulus to work is involved that does not have any achievement-related relevance — as in the case of special "time off" in an officers' training school — the correlation between achievement motivation and performance disappears (French, 1955b).

Achievement-related arousal has little or no effect on women undergraduates if it does not correspond to their preferred value orientation (intellectual role versus women's role) (French & Lesser, 1964; see p. 18). Arousal of curiosity may also obliterate the influence of achievement motivation. In a complex experimental design, Caron (1963) found that success-motivated *S*s (determined on the basis of a combination of *n* Ach and TAQ) comprehended a difficult text better than failure-motivated *S*s of the same intelligence level. This superiority disappears if the *S*s are given to understand at the same time that they will obtain psychological data about themselves that can be better understood with the help of the required reading.

Conversely, arousal may be so strong that differences in potential motivation are obviously overshadowed and evened out by the situational pressure. Required maximum effort in mental arithmetic (with individually assigned speeds) levels out the effects of individual differences in motivation and causes the disappearance of the correlation between arithmetic performance and achievement motivation (Wendt, 1955; Mücher & Heckhausen, 1962; cf. Heckhausen, 1963b, p. 229). McKeachie (1961) found a correlation between school achievement and achievement motivation (*n* Ach) only in students in college courses who were not under achievement pressure, i.e., in courses in which the instructor's style of teaching was not extremely achievement-oriented. Birney (1958b) found that correlations between achievement motivation and performance on arithmetic and coding tasks disappeared if the experiment was conducted by a recognized faculty member and not by an older fellow student.

While the works cited investigated extremes in motive arousal, in which it was either too strong or too weak, other findings should now be cited that were obtained with a degree of arousal between the two extremes that was adequate to produce a recognizable interaction with potential achievement motivation. Highly motivated (*n* Ach) Ss are more self-confident in contrast to Ss with lower motivation when they set an initial goal for a new task for which they do not know their performance capabilities (Pottharst, 1955; Kausler & Trapp, 1958) or when they estimate their probability of success in a task of moderate difficulty (Feather, 1965a). Even after having become familiar with their limitations, the highly motivated Ss evaluate their prospects more favorably in goal-setting and risk-taking (Atkinson *et al.*, 1960; Brody, 1963; cf. Chapter VIII) but not in estimating their probabilities of success (Feather, 1965a). Their motivation is strongest with moderate prospects of success, to judge from their relatively high estimates of probability of success on the first trial of a new task presented as *moderately difficult* rather than easy (Feather, 1965a; the same holds true for success-motivated Ss); or to judge from achievements attained in solving arithmetic problems (Atkinson, 1958a).[9]

[9] Easter and Murstein (1964) intended to check the effect of moderate probabilities of success on achievement arousal. Their

The announcement of an intelligence test results in expectation of success in success-motivated Ss (HS-FF of AM)
and in expectation of failure in failure-motivated persons
(Ertel, 1964). Highly motivated Ss (n Achievement) try harder
on complex mental arithmetic problems as Wendt found
(1955) using the critical flicker fusion measure as an index
of central activation. Simple addition problems, however,
stimulate only failure-motivated Ss to increased and more
persistent efforts (Heckhausen, 1963b); this is probably because the problems are too simple to threaten them with
failure. Simple perceptual tasks appears to produce a similar
type of arousal. They are executed more quickly by Ss with
low motivation than by highly motivated Ss (Vogel et al.,
1959). Furthermore, highly motivated Ss have a lower recognition threshold for success-related words than they have for
failure-related words (McClelland & Liberman, 1949); both

---

procedure is a model of unenlightened research design because the
effect of situational arousal on TAT scores was both obscured and
generally too intensified by repeated and simultaneous experimental
manipulations. To begin with, the writing of the TAT stories (disliked by the Ss because of previous tests) was represented as a class
competition in "creative ability." This was followed by the announcement of a monetary reward. This caused the arousal of nonachievement-related motives which only served to wipe out the expected effects (cf. Atkinson, 1958a). Finally, the probability of winning was established differently for various test groups. After the
Ss had once more estimated their probability of winning they were
finally allowed to write their TAT stories. Is it worth wondering after
all this why the group with moderate probability of winning did not
display significantly higher n Achievement scores than the group
with the 10% probability of winning? Especially since the authors
did not realize that the hypothesis of Atkinson (1957) they were
testing is valid for success-motivated persons only, and that it has
to be reversed for failure-motivated persons. Similar careless
handling of arousal conditions in the TAT experiment can be found
in other studies (Murstein & Collier, 1962; Murstein, 1963).

thresholds are lower in Ss with high n Ach than in failure-motivated Ss (Moulton *et al.*, 1958).

Finally, investigations should be mentioned that control not only potential motivation but also have varied arousal conditions. Using Zeigarnik's retention quotient (1927), Atkinson (1953) showed that Ss with low motivation—who also seem to be predominantly failure-oriented (based on a subsequent analysis by Moulton, 1958)—develop an increasingly avoidant and defensive attitude with the increasing importance of a task. Measured by the extent to which test conditions (relaxed, neutral, ego-involving) indicate that the noncompletion of a task signifies failure, Ss with low motivation (n Ach, failure-motivated persons) recalled successively fewer uncompleted tasks whereas highly motivated Ss recalled *more* uncompleted tasks. According to Raphelson and Moulton (1958), Ss who fear failure do not engage in tasks for which they receive no information on the threat of failure. Tasks with time pressure are apparently experienced as more burdensome by failure-motivated persons (Bartmann, 1963); at any rate, they work more hastily than success-motivated persons and their performance deteriorates as compared to their performance under conditions free of time pressure. Comparing results on a perceptual motor task performed under noncompetitive-neutral and competitive conditions of motive arousal, Ryan and Lakie (1965) have demonstrated that success-motivated Ss (high in FTI and low in MAS) make significantly greater gains during competition than failure-motivated Ss; the latter perform better under noncompetitive conditions than the former.

Douvan (1956) has shown that the effect of material rewards in activating motivation depends on social class position (cf. also Cameron & Storm, 1965). Money prizes increase the achievement-related valence of tasks considerably for adolescents from the working class; they are of no significance for adolescents from the middle class (as well as for those who despite their origin in the lower social stratum would like to be counted in the middle class, cf. Zazzo, 1963; and Katz, 1964). Thus it seems that in the middle-class subculture the mere prospect of success or failure has sufficient incentive value to arouse achievement motivation. Evaluative dispositions for members of this class are, so to speak, more strongly "internalized" and generalized. This has been confirmed by Hoffman *et al.* (1958).

The works cited are concerned with the apperception of the initial achievement-related situation before the beginning of goal-directed activity. Of course, changes in the original apperception also take place during performance. Feedback on the progress of the activity has varying reinforcing effects on the original "demand character" of the task (cf. French, 1958b; see Chapter IX, this volume).

II. PSYCHIC DISTANCE BETWEEN A PRESENT AND A FUTURE STATE

Psychic distance is the other determinant of the expectation gradient. It is determined (a) by the degree of attainability of the goal or the anticipated final state, and (b) by its distance from the present state in time perspective. The *attainability* of the goal depends on the degree of difficulty of the task, which in turn is determined by how it is perceived in relation to one's personal abilities and capabilities. If attainability depends on factors that lie outside a person's possibilities of action and influence (factors such as "chance," "good luck and bad," "orneriness of the subject matter" or the good will or ill will of others), then this is considered a special case. In this instance, it is a question of degrees of attainability whose transitions into the achievement-related area are quite fluid (cf. Feather, 1959a; Mehl, 1962). Attainability as psychic distance to the goal should not be confused with psychic reality, although the two coincide in their extremes. Thus, striving for something unattainable generally includes a level of psychic reality that might be called the "Wish Reality." Something difficult to attain, however, does not have to be experienced as any less real than something that is easy to attain.

How do various degrees of attainability influence the valence of performance goals? As long as all other determinants of the expectation gradient remain constant, increasing the attainability of a goal strengthens its valence or heightens the expectation gradient. This conclusion is a seeming contradiction of the experimentally confirmed fact that it is not the safest enterprises, the easiest tasks, but those with moderate probability of success or a moderate degree of uncertainty about the outcome, that excite the strongest motivation (Hoppe, 1930; Atkinson, 1957, 1958a; Atkinson et al., 1960; Feather, 1959b; McClelland, 1961, p. 218; Heckhausen, 1963b; Brody, 1963; et al.). This apparent paradox can be traced back to the fact that the degree of attainability of a goal does not vary independently of the other determinants of the expectation gradient: as a rule diminishing the degree of attainability of a goal increases the incentive value of the task, its personal importance to the S (Cartwright, 1942; Festinger, 1942; Atkinson, 1957; Feather, 1959a). Feather has shown that the situational conditions in which the task is imbedded are important in this connection—whether it is a matter, for instance, of mere estimates of relative value, of the choice of performance goals, of outcomes which depend on achievement or chance, of real or make-believe tasks. It is important whether the task was chosen or assigned (Greenbaum, Cohn, & Krauss, 1965). A task that was chosen became more attractive and an assigned task less attractive after failure; a fact which can be predicted from Festinger's (1957) Theory of Cognitive Dissonance.

As to the interaction of degree of attainability with motive potential, only the following need be stated here (more details are given in Chapter VIII). Highly motivated Ss and Ss with success-motivation are most strongly motivated by tasks in the area of moderate difficulty with a probability of success of between 30 and 50%. Failure-motivated persons are motivated more strongly by tasks that are either very easy or very difficult; and proportionately more so by the latter if total motivation is higher. These findings were obtained with various methods in several investigations concerning goal setting (Atkinson, 1958a; Atkinson et al., 1960; Atkinson & Litwin, 1960; Heckhausen, 1963b; Brody, 1963) as well as in a study of persistence (Feather, 1961). As to goals whose attainment depends on luck, as in games of chance, the findings were partly similar (Atkinson et al., 1960) and partly different in the sense that success-motivated persons preferred the safest odds and failure-motivated persons preferred the most risky odds (Littig, 1959, 1963b; Feather, 1959a; Hancock & Teevan, 1964). The differences can be explained by the situations in which the tasks were imbedded. Feather (1959a) was able to establish that the inverse relationship between probability of success and motive arousal disappears if judgments of the outcome of events depend on chance more than on one's own ability, and if the choice is imaginary or has less personal significance. In such cases, increasing difficulty no longer produces increased motive arousal.

Finally, if the task involves choosing a partner from a group of persons of varying degrees of ability, one's own motivational level influences the preference for degrees of (here social) attainability (Rosenfeld, 1964). If the other person is more able than oneself, the degree of attainability of winning him as collaborator is perceived as proportionately lower. Nevertheless, success-motivated persons (n Ach and

TAQ) do not choose, as do failure-motivated persons, a partner who is just as able as they are but rather one who is more able; in other words, they prefer lower degrees of attainability (choose what is perceived as more difficult to obtain) in an achievement-related selection of partner (cf. French, 1956).

Another determinant of psychic distance is the length of *time in prospect* between a present and a future state that is anticipated as the goal or end state. In contrast with attainability of the goal, this time interval seems to be relatively independent of the other determinants of the expectation gradient. If the latter are kept constant, the valence of the goal, or the degree of motive arousal, will increase as the goal is approached in time. This is one of those obvious experiments that has not as yet been carried out because the results seem to be self-evident (however, it has recently been performed by Epstein, 1962, for other motives). One of the difficulties involved is the measuring in phenomenologically comparable units distances away in time of goals of different persons. [See, for instance, the varying distance estimates of past and future events by Ss with high and low levels of motivation (Green & Knapp, 1959)].

Some investigations have been concerned with the interaction of motive levels and the extent of future time perspective (cf. above, p. 43). Since highly motivated and success-motivated Ss show a longer range of future time perspective in their achievement-related experiences than do failure-motivated Ss or Ss with low motivation (Heckhausen, 1960, 1963b; Ricks & Epley, in McClelland, 1961), it can be assumed that goals distant in time also have a greater valence for the former than for the latter. Götzl's finding (1960, in Heckhausen, 1963b) can be explained in this way: he showed that success-motivated Ss recall better tasks to be reported on later as compared with closer in time, in contrast to failure-motivated Ss; the above explanation also applies to Mischel's

(1961) finding that highly motivated Ss have more tolerance than Ss with low motivation for longer delays of rewards (see Davids & Sidman, 1962; Strauss, 1962; and Cameron & Storm, 1965).

Substitute value and *achievement fantasies* constitute two special characteristics of the arousal situation that bear on the subject of psychic distance. We have already discussed these phenomena in another connection. Therefore, only the following need be added here: substitute value corresponds to the degree to which the arousal content (valence) of *other* activities or goals coincides with the arousal content of the activities initially undertaken, or the goals initially pursued, which for intrinsic or extrinsic reasons have to be abandoned temporarily or for good. If it is not possible to concretize achievement-oriented undertakings, achievement fantasies may result, i.e., achievement-related projects that lie in the plane of unreality. The substitute (compensatory) value of achievement fantasies is small. As pointed out previously, their significance lies in the anticipation of future phases in performance which at present cannot be realized. This may cause the achievement-related valence of the entire perform-ance, and thus of the present existing phase, to change, i.e., to increase or diminish.

CHAPTER VIII

GOAL SETTING AND LEVEL OF ASPIRATION

The apperception of the situation in the foreperiod is sometimes concluded by goal setting. Goal setting as a phenomenon is not easily isolated for study because a general goal-directedness of the motivating expectation gradient is unmistakable even without explicit goal setting, and because general goal-directedness guides and delimits experience during the apperceptive foreperiod as well as well as during the instrumental or performance period. Even without phenomenal or apperceptive representation, goal-directedness shows itself in the orderly and appropriate succession of cognitive and motor processes.

I. DEFINITIONS

In most cases, therefore, explicit goal setting would be a superfluous act of consciousness. The direction of performance, its objective or goal, and the degrees of excellence connected with it are all implicit in the behavior of a motivated person and can all be determined without taking the trouble to question the person, for instance. There are, however, cases in which explicit goal setting constitutes the natural termination of the foreperiod; namely, when several possible goals or modes of action present themselves and thus

necessitate a *choice,* or a *decision,* or when the future performance phase appears to be specially difficult or unsafe for
various reasons (e.g., after previous failure or if long time
spans have to be bridged or intricately scheduled). In such
cases, goal setting seems to represent a technique for securing
and insuring the attainment of the goal by an act of *intention.*
(Compare the phenomenon of the "complete act of will" —
"Vollständige Willenshandlung" — after Lewin, 1926.) Finally,
a compromise between achievement-related and other projects may also be expressed in goal setting.

In such cases, goal setting explicitly formulates the result
of choices, decisions, schemes, and plans that are designed to
resolve, or at least to order and simplify in concrete fashion,
the many conflicting possibilities of goals and actions apperceived in the foreperiod. Goal setting (also recently labeled
"risk-taking" in English) in this sense is today used in-
admissibly as a synonym for level of aspiration. The reason
for this confusion lies in the experimental practice which has
been followed in procuring level of aspiration data. Before
the execution of the task the *E* asks for an announcement of
the goal sought and thus makes the *S* set an explicit goal. In
his original work (1930), Hoppe was still trying to infer level
of aspiration from the observation of behavior. Behavior dis-
plays no less distinctive characteristics than goal setting as
long as performance is exclusively achievement-motivated.
These characteristics can be observed in a variety of ways
during performance and after its conclusion: in the increased
or diminished effort in the face of changing difficulties; in
the abandonment or pursuit of new solutions; in the expression of affect concerning success and failure; in the
execution or nonexecution of the task; in conflict behavior;
and in expressed expectations of success and failure.

It is customary to understand level of aspiration as the
defined, absolute level of the goal pursued in performing a
given task. The shifting of successively set goals was originally

considered almost exclusively a function of varying levels of performance. The "Laws of Shifting" (upward after success and downward after failure), however, are not too meaningful from the point of view of motivational psychology. They only clarify intraindividual variance in establishing frames of reference for representing degrees of difficulty of a task and degrees of excellence in mastering it. (Changes in the frame of reference after success and failure have been obtained, for instance, by Schmidt & Zarn, 1964.) These are processes of a more cognitive order that create frames of reference from which the motivational ones derive. Insofar as motivational psychology is concerned, it is more productive to understand level of aspiration not as an absolute but rather as a *relatively* defined goal, as a variation in the goal related to attained performance level ("Goal Discrepancy"). Since it has been shown that goal discrepancy is relatively constant within individuals but varies among individuals, it therefore fulfills the conditions of a characteristic of stable motivational differences among individuals.

Level of aspiration in this sense represents a degree of excellence which deviates in direction and level from the performance level that has been reached—a degree of excellence which represents both the goal of performance and effort employed to attain it so that success, or at least not failure, will be experienced. [Rotter (1954) speaks of a "minimum goal."] The "degree of excellence" is experienced as a compulsory "claim" on oneself whether it is in the form of a requirement set by the task, by the need for self-actualization, or by an accepted social norm. The attainment or nonattainment of the "degree of excellence" set affects self-esteem. Thus, an essential element in stable evaluative dispositions finds expression in the concrete level of aspiration stated in a given situation (cf. Chapter III). Furthermore, it should be noted that the level of aspiration is not merely an achievement-related phenomenon. We find it in all person-environment relationships which, in one way or another, affect self-esteem and thereby norms that are organized apperceptively around ethical, political, social, economic, or social prestige matters.

II. RESULTS AND THEORETICAL REVIEW

The results of the research on level of aspiration up to the present can be summarized as follows:

1. The experience of success and failure is not tied to objective (i.e., the same for different people) characteristics of the task but rather to the degree of difficulty the task represents within the experience of one's own achievement-related abilities. The personal level of difficulty for tasks corresponds to the personal degree of excellence of one's own achievements.

2. Success and failure is experienced only within an area of moderate (subjective) difficulty. The closer a completed task lies to the upper level of the area of moderate difficulty, the more success is experienced; and the closer an uncompleted task lies to the lower limit of the area of difficulty, the more failure is experienced.

3. There is a general tendency (evaluative disposition, especially its success-motivated portion) to push one's own ability to achieve upward, as measured by the *objective* difficulty of the task. This involves shifting and redefining one's own measure of difficulty (and the related level of excellence of one's own achievement) in relation to an objective measure of difficulty: something previously appearing difficult now appears to be easy (or vice versa).

4. There are personal preferences for levels of difficulty, or for degrees of excellence in one's own performance. This is the level of aspiration in the sense of the previously mentioned discrepancy of the goal from the performance level attained (which is usually understood to mean equal probability of

success or failure in a repeat performance). The level of aspiration states the preference for either a 50:50 risk of failure (in agreement with the performance level attained), or for a slightly to greatly increased, or for a decreased risk ("risk-taking," cf. p. 95). Individual variability in the level of aspiration, which was noted earlier, is an expression of achievement motivation and constitutes an important element in achievement-related evaluative dispositions. The preferred level of aspiration lies outside the area of moderate difficulty in extreme cases; it is set too low or too high. Goal setting in these extreme areas is more rigid and not as flexible as it is in the area of moderate difficulty. Even if the performance level shifts, the goals set are not changed immediately. This results in a certain fluctuation of the level of aspiration (as goal discrepancy.)

5. The objective level of aspiration is not only a function of the evaluative disposition consisting of what "ought to be" (including the variations on it resulting from rigid goal setting). There is also intraindividual variance resulting from situational factors. The level of aspiration may, therefore, be defined as an *area* of degrees of excellence with boundaries at a lower and an upper level. Situational factors include at least the following four: the importance of the task; the level of reality of the task or the goal setting; the distance away in time of the task to be performed or of the attainment of the goal; and the conflict between achievement-related standards of excellence of various types.

The schematic diagram in Fig. 1 illustrates the five main points of the research results up to the present time. (1) The marks on the edges of Column I represent different levels of difficulty of task X. The experience of success and failure is not fixed at the absolute level of difficulty but depends on the personal standard of difficulty of task X (Column II, for which the marks representing difficulty level are set to correspond roughly to the objective difficulty levels), or on the related level of excellence of one's achievement (Column III). (2) achievement level (Ach L) attained at any given time is surrounded by an area of difficulty of personal relevance of a given width which is limited by the too difficult at the top and the too easy at the bottom. Compare the horizontal dotted

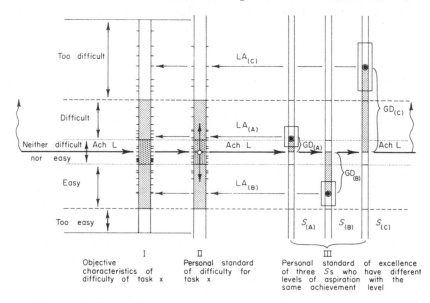

FIG. 1.   Differing levels of aspiration (LA) for equal achievement levels (Ach L), i.e. with equal levels of mastery of task X (I) and equal personal standards of difficulty for this task (II). The personal standards of excellence for subjects A, B, and C (III) vary in extent and direction from the achievement level attained as to the degree of excellence experienced as obligatory (i.e., their level of aspiration). The deviation is the personal goal discrepancy (GD) which is an expression of achievement-related evaluative dispositions.

lines, the shaded portions of Columns I and II, and the description at the left. (3) The general tendency to make an effort to improve one's own performance is indicated by the winding arrows which start upward from the existing achievement level. If performance changes after efforts to improve it, personal standards of difficulty and of what constitutes excellence in relation to objective levels of difficulty (I) are then set in motion. The standards swing upward when performance improves and downward when it gets worse. This is indicated by the double arrow in Column II. (4) Different Ss (A, B, C) may have differing levels of aspiration (LA) even though their achievement levels (Ach L) and the corresponding personal standards of excellence (III) are the same. The arrows pointing to Column I indicate the choice of a definite goal in terms of the objective scale of difficulty of the task. As a result of factors not represented in the figure, subjects A, B, and C have different evaluative dispositions which show up in differences both in the size and direction of their goal discrepancies (GD, shaded portions of column III) as well as in the different levels of aspiration set (represented by double circles). (5) The variation in levels of aspiration, caused by situational factors (as well as by the fluctuation in goal discrepancy from rigid goal setting) is indicated by the frames around the preferred levels of aspiration (double circles). The extent of these areas of fluctuation in goal discrepancies varies among persons (see subjects A, B, and C) and probably increases with more extreme levels of aspiration.

The latter condition has hardly been considered up to the present as a part of the problem of clarifying intraindividual variation in levels of aspiration. The effects of the first four factors have been investigated only occasionally. If the task has greater importance (ego involvement), the level of aspiration rises somewhat (J. D. Frank, 1935; Feather, 1959a; Ferguson, 1962; Diggory & Morlock, 1964) but it also then varies less closely with changing performance level (Feather, 1959b). Level of aspiration also tends to rise slightly if goal setting is done at a more unreal level (if the goal is "desired," not "expected") (Festinger, 1942; Irwin, 1944; Feather, 1959a). Conflicts between task-related and social standards of excellence may be expressed in so-called "split" levels of aspiration (Heckhausen, 1955), i.e., in low settings of announced goals versus higher ones kept for oneself. The effect of distance away in time perspective, finally, has apparently been little researched up to the present time. Diggory and Morlock (1964) have studied experimentally two standards of excellence of different origin along with the effects of a fixed time limit provided for the attainment of a goal; they used a test situation which was quite true to life with respect to the achievement requirements of school and career. In addition to observing his own improvement in performance, the S was compelled by the E to orient himself toward a very high level of excellence which had to be reached after ten separate tests. Under such limited conditions of choice, goal setting was determined by one's own improvement in performance; the perceived probability of success in attaining the final imposed goal was, however, determined by the discrepancy still remaining between the attained and the required final level of performance, and by the nearness in time of the conclusion of the experiment, when the final goal was supposed to be reached.

Research on level of aspiration has, however, been mainly preoccupied with the first three points mentioned. It has been concerned with shifts in goals depending on the experience of success or failure with the same or similar tasks, and it has been concerned with information provided in terms of other frames of reference such as the announcement of achievement norms for various reference groups (cf. the only over-all review: Lewin *et al.*, 1944). This really involves only how personal standards of difficulty (or their corresponding standards for excellence of performance) are set up or altered in relation to the objective difficulty of the task.

However, from the viewpoint of the psychology of motivation, the issues involved in point 4 were raised quite early since they dealt with individual differences in levels of aspiration resulting from variations in personal standards of difficulty or of excellence of performance. Large individual variations in the height of the level of aspiration are accompanied by rather stable discrepancies between goals attained and goals set (GD) within the individual. Mehl (1962, p. 248) found this to be true even with abruptly induced experiences of success and failure. Heckhausen and Wagner (1965) were able to establish even in 4½ -year-old children intraindividual consistency in goal setting involved in tasks of strength and skill. The same is true, too, for McClelland's (1958a) ring-tossing experiment with 5-year-olds whose preferred distance in tossing rings correlated with an independent index of achievement motivation (based on Aronson, 1958). In short, goal discrepancies seem to be stable indicators of motivational characteristics whereas levels of aspiration while related to motivation are also complexly determined by cognitive factors.

III. RELATIONSHIP OF GOAL SETTING TO MOTIVATION

J. D. Frank (1935) is of the opinion that various motivational tendencies operate with differing weights from one person to another. Accordingly, level of aspiration is a result of a conflict among the following needs: (a) to choose a high level of difficulty in order to achieve maximum success; (b) to choose a low level of difficulty in order to meet with as little failure as possible; and (c) to choose a moderate level of difficulty whose mastery still appears possible and whose outcome one is most likely to predict exactly. The reality of these motivational tendencies was supported by questionnaire data (Frank, 1938), by observation of behavior, and by a postperformance interview (Heckhausen, 1955). The analysis of the relationships involved requires, furthermore, the isolation of the enduring motivation tendencies which appear to be of importance for the level of aspiration of a person and which can be measured apart from the goal setting procedure itself. The requirement of separate measurement has been fulfilled in many investigations with all sorts of personality variables (e.g., Gould & Kaplan, 1940; Gardner, 1940; Eysenck, 1947; Zelen, 1954; Guérin, 1958; Scodel et al., 1959); however, the requirement of isolation of a key motivational tendency has been met only through the assessment of achievement motivation via the TAT method. Nevertheless, Pauline S. Sears anticipated the principal features of the more recent results as early as 1940. She used 10- and 12-year-old S s who were pupils striving for high achievement. Based on their standing in school, she divided them into success and failure groups, thus, obviously according to whether success or failure motivation predominated. Successful pupils preferred to set realistic, moderate goals while unsuccessful pupils selected either speculatively extreme or overcautiously low goals (cf. Jucknat, 1937).

The basic nature of the relationship between achievement motivation and level of aspiration has been confirmed again and again in more recent investigations. This is highly remarkable because the nature and strength of achievement motivation was measured by various methods, and because the tasks and other test conditions involved had little in common in these investigations. Among the first studies using the n Achievement method is Martire's (1956) in which highly motivated persons with fear of failure and strong conflict (i.e., persons who produce much achievement apperception after little arousal and little achievement apperception after strong arousal on the TAT) set cautiously low goals. In an investigation by Clark et al. (1956) involving undergraduates about to take an examination, highly motivated S s, who appeared to be predominantly success-motivated based on TAT findings, set moderate goals for a test they were about to take and for certain other questionnaire criteria while S s with lower motivation tended rather to underestimate or overestimate their prospects of success in an unrealistic way. Reitman and Williams (1961), however, were not able to confirm the relations found between Clark's level of aspiration questionnaire and achievement motivation.

McClelland (1958a) was the first to observe characteristic differences in tasks chosen when they require skill. Five- to nine-year-old children more frequently chose moderately difficult tasks in a ring-tossing game if they were highly motivated (as measured by the Aronson method, 1958). They chose distances from which only about every third toss would succeed. Using college students in a ring-tossing game, Litwin (1958) and Atkinson and Litwin (1960) were able to demonstrate a similar result, as were Atkinson *et al.* (1960) in a game of shuffleboard. Success-motivated persons (FTI and TAQ combined) prefer moderate distances more than failure-motivated persons. Smith (1963) obtained the same result with intelligence test problems in an ascending order of difficulty; however, his results were obtained only under relaxed and not under neutral test conditions. According to Isaacson (1964) the same model of preference in the choice of difficulty can also be found outside the laboratory situation, namely, in the choice of college courses. Success-motivated students (*n* Achievement and TAQ) prefer courses of moderate difficulty while failure-motivated students prefer either very difficult or very easy courses. (It was not possible to confirm this with women undergraduates.)

Career goals have also been used as indicators of level of aspiration. Mahone (1960) found that failure-motivated adolescents make more unrealistic career choices than do success-motivated adolescents. The career choices are either above or below their ability to achieve them. Using Clark and co-workers' (1956) questionnaire method, Burnstein (1963) investigated the extent to which desired careers are seriously aspired to. Success-motivated persons (*n* Achievement and TAQ) have a higher level of aspiration than do failure-motivated persons in this regard. The latter display withdrawal tendencies and are content with simpler occupations if it means evading the uncertainties and exertions involved in a more demanding career. (Littig, 1963a, and Rim, 1963, have confirmed this with other methods.) Simultaneously, however, in their thoughts they reach out more for practically unattainable occupations than do success-motivated persons. Minor and Neel (1958) proved that highly motivated persons throughout have a higher occupational level of aspiration. In this respect, the demands for one's best performance are more decisive than the mere prestige of an occupation, according to Burnstein *et al.* (1963; see also Morgan, 1964).

High achievement motivation does lead to entering entrepreneurial occupations as McClelland (1965b) found in a longitudinal study over 10 to 14 years. According to his theory of economic development (1961), highly motivated males can satisfy their achievement aspirations better in business jobs of an entrepreneurial nature in which decision-making should be based on moderate, calculated risks (cf. below; Meyer *et al.*, 1961). Lambert and Klineberg (1963) have found in a cross-national study that boys' career aspirations are higher in countries with higher *n* Achievement, as measured by content analysis of children's readers.

Robinson (1962a) has taken off from Sears' (1940) original study and attempted to clarify the relationship further between school achievement and level of aspiration by taking achievement motivation into account. Successful 11- to 12-year-old pupils set, in comparison with their last performance, rather slightly increased, albeit not unrealistic, goals, while the failure group leaned toward either overly high or overly low levels of aspiration. Pupils from the group with moderate levels of aspiration displayed higher *n* Achievement scores (and based more on success-oriented content) than the others did (cf. Robinson, 1962b).

In part, it has been possible to obtain the same results even if goal setting is not in an achievement-related setting but involves only *choices of risks with respect to outcomes depending on chance.* Atkinson *et al.* (1960) found that highly motivated persons (*n* Achievement) more frequently prefer moderate risks in imaginary games of chance *when compared* to *S*s with low *n* Achievement who tend to avoid intermediate risks; however, this is true only as long as a stake of (fictitious) money is not involved. Litwin (1958) was able to confirm the same preference for moderate risk in a game of horse racing. Littig (1959, 1963b) observed that highly motivated and success-motivated persons behave differently if a stake of real money is involved and the outcome depends on chance. They prefer the least risk or the greatest probability of winning. Hancock and Teevan (1964) report similar findings. Success-motivated college students choose the safest odds with the lowest money returns in playing a slot machine; failure-motivated students chose the riskiest odds with the highest winnings. The latter are in general more "irrational" in their choices, i.e., they fluctuate more in the choice of chances for a lucky break. (The motivational measure used here was the TAT scoring key "Hostile Press" developed by Birney *et al.*, 1961, for the scoring of fear of failure.) In a carefully controlled study Raynor and Smith (1965) have found clear evidence that high *n* Ach *S*s as well as success-motivated *S*s (high *n* Ach–low TAQ) prefer intermediate risks in a game of skill but not in a game of pure chance. The relationship for the game of skill is stronger under achievement-oriented conditions than under relaxed conditions. Based on McClelland's (1961) expectations, Meyer *et al.* (1961) have tested the preferences of *S*s in entrepreneurial positions for moderate risks. Managers in such positions have, as expected, greater achievement motivation than comparable specialists and choose more moderate risks more often out of a variety of betting odds. Brody (1963) used a task of sequential decision-making in which the outcome was less dependent on chance than are risks in betting. Success-motivated persons (*n* Achievement and TAQ) preferred moderate risks while failure-motivated persons preferred extremely low or high risks. (Compare Section II, Risk Taking, in Chapter V.)

Feather (1961, 1963b) was also able to establish the same relationship between motivation and level of aspiration in an instance in which the level of aspiration was not determined from announced goal settings but rather from observed behavior, namely, from the time it took for an *S* to abandon a task which at first appeared to be solvable, yet defied all efforts. Success-motivated persons persevered longer than failure-motivated persons if the task was originally passed off as easy; however, the latter persevered longer than the former if the task was announced as difficult at the start. These differences are explained by the preference of success-motivated persons for tasks of moderate difficulty and the preference of failure-motivated persons for tasks of extreme difficulty. A task, appearing easily solvable at first (but actually unsolvable), assumes the character of moderate difficulty early in the course of experiencing difficulties with it. Since moderate difficulty is preferred by success-motivated persons and avoided by failure-motivated persons, the latter resign after a short time of trying. Correspondingly, the reverse is true if the task appears to be very difficult from the start for in the course of time it quickly approaches the area of extreme difficulty which is avoided by success-motivated persons.

Smith (1964) was able to confirm the same relationship with respect to the time used by success-motivated persons to finish a written exam. If they considered the exam to be easy, the more success-motivated (FTI and TAQ) they were the less time they spent on it; however, if it appeared to be moderately difficult they tried that much longer, in an exact reversal of their previous behavior.

Finally, it has also been possible to demonstrate the preference of highly motivated S s for moderate prospects of success on the basis of another measure, namely, actual performance. With a probability of success of only 33% (in competing in a group of three to win an announced prize), highly motivated S s performed better on an arithmetic test than did S s with low motivation; in other words, the former seemed to work harder when prospects of success were only moderately high (Atkinson, 1958a). Success-motivated S s (high n Ach—low TAQ) working at a difficult anagrams task obtained higher performance scores if the initial expectation of success was moderately low compared to high initial expectations of success (Feather, 1965b).

Recently, Moulton (1965) was able to exercise stricter control over the subjective probabilities of success. He managed this at the expense of the range of free choice in goal setting. Subjects were seen individually and had to choose between an easy, intermediate, or difficult task (25, 50, or 75% of subjective probability of success, respectively, depending on the individual's pretest score in a related ability test). Irrespective of their preference, all S s were made to start with the task of intermediate difficulty, at the end of which S s who initially had chosen the easy task were told that they had failed and those who had chosen the difficulty task were told that they had succeeded. By this experimental device the initially symmetrical range of difficulties is unbalanced in one direction or the other, and either the initially preferred easy or difficult task now comes closer to the 50% level of difficulty. According to Atkinson's risk-taking model (1957), it was expected that the more failure-motivated rather than success-motivated S s would shift over from their initial choice to the other extreme in order to avoid the area of even odds as far as possible (cf. Feather, 1961, 1963b; see p. 96). In level of aspiration terms this means an atypical reaction to success and failure experiences, viz., setting a higher goal after failure and lower goal after success. The results show that only a minority of all Ss reacted in this atypical manner, but this minority comprised significantly more people with predominant failure- than success-motivation. It cannot be concluded definitely from this and other findings that the author has shown that failure-motivated persons generally tend to shift atypically in goal-setting after success and failure experiences, for the possibilities of choice were heavily restricted. The unbalanced trio of task difficulties did not permit the subject to move out of the area of even odds in the "typical" direction.

The latest and up to now the most satisfactory technique of measuring preferred probabilities of success in a task of skill (shooting a ball in a basket) has been proposed by DeCharms and Davé (1965). The Ss practiced initially over an evenly distributed range of distances. The actual probabilities of success for each distance were then calculated and shown to the S before he was given his free choices as to where to stand. Running the Ss individually in this way provided in- dividual standards of proficiency uncontaminated by group standards, which have influenced the results in earlier studies (Atkinson & Litwin, 1960; Atkinson et al., 1960). The mean probabilities of success preferred by each S could thus be fairly compared because the effects of individual differences in proficiency had been eliminated. The average probability of success preferred by all Ss was .34 (about 1 chance in 3 of succeeding), a value which corresponds to what has been ob- tained in earlier studies and which the authors consider the point of "moderate risk probability." They then calculated a deviation score consisting of the average deviation of the individual's chosen levels of probability on 20 shots from the group mean. Their results did not replicate the usual finding that Ss with high n Achievement and low Test Anxiety show a greater preference for moderately high goals. Using a modifi- cation of the n Achievement scoring key to distinguish be-

tween Hope of Success and Fear of Failure, they found that
Ss high on *both* measures preferred moderately high goals
more. It is possible to explain their unexpected results. For
instance, employing the usual TAT method in a group testing
session might not be appropriate for the age group studied
(10–12 years of age).

The works cited (with the exception of Clark *et al.*, 1956 and
McClelland, 1958a) were stimulated by Atkinson's model
(1957) of risk-taking, or goal-setting, behavior. This model is
an expansion of the so-called "Resultant Valence Theory"
with which Escalona (1940) and Festinger (1942) attempted
to explain the setting of level of aspiration. To the two variables of incentive value and probability of success of a task
(which vary inversely), Atkinson added a motivational variable
consisting of the extent to which success motivation or failure
motivation predominated. He made the first two variables
complementary so that they would add up to 1.00 and combined all three variables in a multiplicative function. In this
way the highest "motivation value" (.25) is obtained with
moderate probability of success (.50) and moderate incentive
value (.50); in other words, such a task has the highest attrac-
tion for success-motivated persons. It has the highest valence.
Since, in the case of predominant failure motivation, the
resultant product would receive a negative sign (because the
probability of failure is multiplied with "negative" incentive
value, i.e., the degree of failure threat of the task), failure-
motivated persons avoid most tasks of moderate difficulty.
(Compare Atkinson's summarizing statement, 1964, p. 240–
268.)

Atkinson's theory appears to be mathematized calculus
rather than a psychological model. Since a rigid complementary relationship between incentive and probability of success
is presupposed, two of the three variables need not be obtained independently. Nevertheless, the theory has proven

extremely fruitful in stimulating research.[10] The calculus has "predictive" value insofar as it allows the inference that failure-motivated Ss prefer the outside limits of an area of possible goal settings, while success-motivated Ss prefer an "in between" area. This "in between" area, however, does not coincide with a moderate probability of success of about 50% as it should according to the calculus. On the contrary, success-motivated persons tend to prefer lower to medium probabilities of success; in other words, slightly higher goals with success probabilities of around 1 in 3. DeCharms and Davé (1965), in the study just cited, have shown that for all Ss the value can be as low as .34. Atkinson (1957, 1958a) attempted to explain this deviation from his calculations by the fact that success-motivated persons overestimate their ability to perform as long as they have not attempted the new task (Pottharst, 1955; Kausler & Trapp, 1958; Atkinson et al., 1960). Compared with Ss who fear failure (Feather, 1963a, using AAT) or who have low motivation (Brody, 1963; Feather, 1965a), they tend to have higher estimates of their initial probabilities of success. Yet under the reality constraints of the first practice trials their *probability estimates* increasingly correlate with task performance and no longer with predominant success or failure motivation (Feather, 1965a). In contrast

---

[10] In the meantime a new elaboration of the theory involves the introduction of the construct of "inertial tendencies." It takes into account the persistent effect of previously aroused but unsatisfied behavioral tendencies (Atkinson & Cartwright, 1964). Quite recently, Weiner (1965b) added a further refinement which seems to offer an improvement in the theory's predictive power. In this modified approach, Weiner considers the effects of previous success or failure in interaction with predominant success or failure motivation. This includes the effects on resumption of incompleted tasks (Weiner, 1965a), choice between achievement- and nonachievement-related activities (Weiner & Rosenbaum, 1965), and learning of easy and complex tasks (Weiner, 1966).

to this, they continue to set slightly higher goals even if they have gained sufficient experience as to their actual performance. This has been shown repeatedly (e.g., McClelland, 1958a), especially by Atkinson and his associates (Litwin, 1958; Littig, 1959; Atkinson *et al.*, 1960). Atkinson and Litwin (1960) report that success-motivated persons (*n* Achievement and TAQ) prefer an average (objective) probability of success of 23% in the ring-tossing game. The achievement-related choice of work partners has shown similar results (Rosenfeld, 1964, cf. above, p. 79).

Heckhausen was able to confirm the result in his investigations (1958, 1963b with a detailed discussion of Atkinson's theory; cf. McClelland, 1961, pp. 223 ff). Success-motivated college students set moderate to fairly high goals while failure-motivated students set either moderately low or extremely high goals in individual tasks involving maze learning and in group tasks involving simple tests of addition. Meyer *et al.* (1065, on the basis of AM) found the same to be true for 9-year-old pupils. Figure 1 (see p. 88) illustrates the three typical cases of level of aspiration setting with different directions and varying discrepancies from the performance level attained (i.e., a moderate probability of success of 50%) in subjects A, B, and C. No explanation is needed for the fact that failure-motivated persons set a goal that lies below their last performance, i.e., one that can certainly be attained (cf. subject B, Fig. 1). It is surprising, however, that subject C chooses an utterly extreme goal that cannot be attained. The reckless group of failure-motivated persons can be distinguished from the cautious group by a higher total motivation score (HS + FF). Characteristic differences also appear in a comparison of the TAT stories from a clinically diagnostic point of view; those of the first group frequently contain obstacles and setbacks in performance which the main protagonist incessantly tries to overcome; the stories of the second group frequently contain interruptions in achievement efforts, rest periods, and withdrawals. The differences correspond to the way the two groups perform and set goals. As has been found earlier (Heckhausen, 1955), persons setting extremely high goals are guided by high-flying desires for success and are thoroughly confident. Furthermore, they stand out because of extraordinary effort. It need not be a paradox to discover their enduring achievement motivation level is nevertheless failure- and not success-oriented when one takes into consideration that their perception and behavior in the level of aspiration test is an attempt to resolve a conflict between approach and avoidance tendencies. The conflict is softened by the intensification of approach tendencies, by a "frontal breakthrough." A further expression of this desire to avoid conflict is rigid goal setting in the face of failure.

Cohen and Zimbardo (1962) have also found such behavior in situationally produced conflict and explained it in the framework of cognitive dissonance theory. Steiner's (1957) finding is also illuminating; he found that setting very high goals is correlated with an uncertain self-image, while setting low goals is associated with a pessimistic self-image (cf. Gardner, 1940; and Martire, 1956). Argyle and Robinson (1962) found that the extent of achievement-related demands on oneself (as one "should" be) correlates with the strength of fear of failure (negative categories of the n Achievement measure).

The motivation of success-motivated Ss, for whom moderate to slightly elevated goal setting is characteristic, is easier to understand. They are guided not only by desires for success but also by a realistic estimation of the probabilities of success. Thus, they prefer maximum uncertainty as to the successful or unsuccessful outcome of their efforts. Success or failure when they have a 50:50 chance of reaching a goal they have set depends to the maximum possible extent on their own competence and expenditure of energy. As McClelland (1961; cf. also Meyer *et al.*, 1961) was able to prove, this neither speculative nor cautious but "calculated" risk-taking is characteristic of the successful entrepreneurial personality. The successful entrepreneur sets goals that are neither ridiculously easy (Subject B, Fig. 1) nor depend too much on lucky external circumstances (Subject C) but depend maximally on one's own competence (Subject A). Two further facts fit this picture well: success-motivated Ss more than failure-motivated Ss tend to lower their goals after failure, and they have a more extended achievement-related future time perspective (Heckhausen, 1963b).

CHAPTER IX

THE PERFORMANCE PERIOD

As in the foreperiod, the nature and extent of motivational arousal by a task can change during the activity itself, thereby controlling the intensity of the expenditure of energy. In the most general sense this is the meaning of the traditional observation that varying difficulties and energy demands of a task result in "exertion of the will" *(Willensanspannung)* or energy output [the so called "Law of Difficulty" in Motivation: *Schwierigkeitsgesetz der Motivation* (Ach, 1910, p. 253; Hillgruber, 1912)]. The relationship between difficulty and energy output is so immediate and without mediating conscious content (cf. the learning studies by Schönpflug, 1963) that it could be cited as a model example of automatic feedback, for which motivating processes in the sense of a perceived or experienced gradient of expectation need not be hypothesized. However, the feedback loop seems to depend on a certain experience of the situation, namely, on an overriding "goal image." This is suggested by Mierke's finding (1955, pp. 52 ff.) to the effect that a hypnotically induced activity is promptly followed by a linear decline in performance on the ergometer and not by scalloped increments in performance produced by drive *(Antriebshebungen)* as is the case with normal "waking" activities. On the other hand, *one single* expenditure of energy after extremely strong suggestion leads to a greater increase in performance in the hypnotic state than it does in the normal waking state (Slotnick, Liebert, & Hilgard, 1965).

Both results are consistent with the idea that a lasting "goal image" is absent in the hypnotic state. We do not want to enter more deeply into the large areas of research that are concerned with the phenomena of exercise, fatigue, exertion, tension, etc. Instead we wish to discuss the three aspects of performance that belong together and are related to achievement motivation, namely (1) activation, (2) the effect of feedback as to success and failure on feelings and expectations about the situation, and (3) persistence.

I. ACTIVATION

Activation and its theoretical interpretation have gained great importance for research on motivation and behavior (Hebb, 1955; Lindsley, 1957; Malmo, 1959; Berlyne, 1960) after the discovery of the functions of the so-called "ascending reticular arousal system" (ARAS) in the lower brain. Anatomic signs such as electric skin resistance, pulse frequency, and muscle tonus are normally used as indicators of central activation. Attempts have also been made to measure activation with the help of anxiety questionnaires (MAS) and of experimentally aroused need states. It has been shown that activation level rises with increasing psychic demands of an activity [measured, for instance, with the electromyogram (Mücher & Heckhausen, 1962)]. The discovery that an inverted U-function characterizes the relationship of activation to excellence of performance as had been foreshadowed by the old Yerkes-Dodson Law (1908) is quite significant. A moderate level of activation is optimal (cf. Surwillo, 1956; Stennet, 1957). What constitutes the optimal level depends on the nature of the task. Thus, performance on simple, sensorimotor tasks improves with increasing activation (Vogel *et al.*, 1959) or with increasing "drive" as Taylor (1956) concluded from performance in a threatening test situation of *S*s with varying scores on an anxiety questionnaire (MAS). On the other hand, a decline in performance on more complex thought problems occurs even with moderately strong activation (e.g., Taylor & Spence, 1952; Mandler & Sarason, 1952; Helm, 1954; Katchmar, Ross, & Andrews, 1958; Nicholson, 1958; Vogel *et al.*, 1959; Sarason, 1961; Ray, 1965).

Insofar as achievement motivation is concerned, highly motivated persons are more highly activated in achievement situations; this has been found using as measurements of activation either the critical flicker fusion frequency (Wendt, 1955) or the resting level of muscle tonus during mental activity and rest periods [(Mücher & Heckhausen, 1962; Heckhausen, 1963b); in this last instance the measurement was not made on the basis of flicker fusion frequency]. Highly motivated persons, in other words, exert themselves more or "mobilize more energy." They also solve more intricate arithmetic tasks when they are left free to pace themselves as they wish (Wendt, 1955); but not when they are constantly prodded (Wendt, 1955) or when they are under pressure to reach an extremely high goal (Mücher & Heckhausen, 1962). Using an exploratory questionnaire, Tent (1963) distinguished between Ss with high and low motivation and obtained their activation levels *(Anspannung)* in solving similar arithmetic problems for more than 3 hours by continuously recording pulse frequency (cf. Bartenwerfer, 1960). He considered changes in pulse frequency over work output an expression of the relative changes in energy output that are experienced during an activity. Highly motivated persons expended more energy; in other words, they made more effort from the start, they began at a higher performance level and, therefore, needed relatively more activation (energy) (in contrast to Ss with low motivation) in order to keep performance level from declining. High activation also affects expressive movements: handwriting of more highly motivated Ss shows greater pressure, is more directed toward the right, and is more expansive (Grünewald & Mücher, 1964). Systolic blood pressure (after

15 minutes of lying down) correlates negatively with success motivation; surprisingly in persons with essential hypertension the correlation is positive (Heckhausen, 1963b).

Varying characteristics of activation in success- and failure-motivated Ss have also been studied with the help of galvanic skin responses (GSR). Raphelson (1957) as well as Raphelson and Moulton (1958) found that success-motivated persons (using n Achievement and TAQ combined) in tasks of sensorimotor coordination initially show a very high level of activation (GSR), which falls off significantly during the activity, while failure-motivated persons begin at a lower level, which, however, rises significantly (Vogel *et al.*, 1958). Success-motivated persons are already highly activated before the E's instructions thus revealing (most probably) their achievement-related apperception of the situation and the tension level of their expectations [or, according to Schlosberg (1954), they may be said to keep more energy mobilized; findings by Vogel *et al.* (1959, p. 232) should be similarly understood]. Subjects high in text anxiety (TAQ) show more violent changes in galvanic skin resistance than less anxious Ss in response to expectations and experiences of failure (Kissel & Littig, 1962), and their performance also deteriorates (Sarason, Mandler, & Craighill, 1952).

A finding by Bartmann (1963) is remarkable in that it shows that activation-increasing stress, such as mild time pressure, has a deteriorating effect on complex thought processes only for failure-motivated persons. It has an advantageous effect for success-motivated persons. Achievement-related situational stress appears to upset failure-motivated persons particularly and to create a "task attitude" (cf. p. 40) which interferes with their ability to function cognitively. Thus R. W. Brown (1953) found with failure-motivated persons (middle-third of the n Achievement distribution) that the readiness to restructure or find shortcuts in the solution of thought problems diminished significantly under ego-involving conditions. If a classroom examination takes place in a relaxed atmosphere, the original inferiority of failure-motivated persons disappears (McKeachie *et al.*, 1955). Mierke (1954, 1955) reported that extreme demands, whether they are induced via extraordinary time pressure, or an extraordinary task difficulty, lead to a regular sequence of reactions. After a short-term breakdown in performance characterized by false starts, a certain level of performance is gradually built up again via an intermediate phase of simple motor reactions. Obviously one could try to explain this sequence in terms of an induced hyperelevation of the level of activation that can only be brought back down slowly to the optimal middle area.

II. FEEDBACK ABOUT SUCCESS AND FAILURE

Changes of activation usually go with changing feelings about the situation, with fluctuating expectations of success and failure, which are aroused by *feedback* about the progress of the activity according to plan. In this sense, activation and changes in the experienced expection gradient are the results of feedback about success and failure. A change in the valence of the task may occur during the performance period as a result of this feedback; even a complete reapperception of the situation may take place such as "going-out-of-the-field" (Lewin, 1926) in the face of threatening experiences or prospects of failure. Under conditions of drastic frustration lasting several hours, Dembo (1931) has demonstrated this with a seemingly solvable task and Helm (1954) with a seemingly easy "intelligence test." Helm intensified the stress of failure by offensive criticism from the *E*. As a result, cognitive functioning deteriorated greatly. It no longer was possible to divide up the task into problems to be solved, and the result was blind test behavior ending with complete thought disintegration [cf. the summary by Lazarus *et al.* (1952)]. Helm

(1958) has proved that increased success feedback also changes the style of work in solving conceptual and construction tasks, namely, in the direction of a "more destructured trial-and-error approach" and a "decrease in an appropriate sense of risk" that results in a favorable or unfavorable outcome depending on the demands of the task.

The patterns of interaction are complex (cf. Heckhausen, 1963b, p. 269 ff.). For example, situational pressure caused by distressing failure experiences may improve the ability of certain persons to function as has been pointed out by Lazarus *et al.* (1952) in their summary review. More recently Alpert and Haber (1960) have taken this fact into account in the construction of their "Achievement Anxiety Test" (AAT) which appears to be the best questionnaire for the measuring of achievement-related anxiety at present. It contains a scale for facilitating and a scale for debilitating anxiety in achievement situations which correlate negatively with each other and, which, when combined, increase the accuracy in predicting school grades (cf. Dember *et al.*, 1962). According to Feather's (1963d) findings, the facilitating anxiety score of the AAT correlates with the prediction of success in the face of increasing failure experience. Failure expectations and fear of failure obviously rise with increasing failure. So it is remarkable that success-motivated persons (using *n* Achievement and AAT) feel less fear than failure-motivated persons do even after experiencing that only one out of every 9 or 10 of their solutions is correct. If feedback about success and failure is omitted, highly motivated persons attain success in a complex task sooner than do persons with low motivation (French & Thomas, 1958).

McKeachie (1961, p. 138) was able to obtain this result also for a normal teaching situation in college courses. Highly motivated students with little achievement anxiety (using AAT) obtained better final grades (and also thought they had learned more) from those teachers who organized their

courses less along achievement lines and who did not try to
activate the students much through frequent feedback about
success and failure. Large amounts of feedback, stimulation,
and even achievement pressure improved the performance
of the Ss with low motivation as long as they were not also
anxious about achievement; for the highly motivated S such
pressure obviously interferes with his spontaneous achievement orientation. Failure-motivated persons may experience
the absence of feedback as so threatening that they "leave
the field" psychologically as Raphelson and Moulton (1958)
concluded from the disappearance of the correlation between
n Achievement and TAQ in this condition and from the
changes in GSR.

Pedagogically useful feedback is especially provided in
so called programmed learning since the teaching machine
reports immediately on the correctness of the separate steps
taken in learning and allows the individual to pace his own
working speed. There is one study so far which shows that
success-motivated persons (HS-FF, AM) are better able to
profit from self-guided learning under such feedback conditions. Bartmann (1965) had 15-year-old students work on insight problems, each working for three periods of 30 minutes
during a 3-week-long programmed instruction period. Success motivation correlated significantly with improvements
in performance between a pretest and a posttest (parallel
forms of the same thought problems); the correlation is entirely independent of differences in intelligence.

Finally, the question should be raised as to what feedback
conditions promote optimal functioning. Some clues exist
for highly motivated persons. With moderate prospects of
success (namely, with a probability of 33% of winning a prize
in competition with others) highly motivated Ss are able to
solve more tasks of mental arithmetic, i.e., they make the
greatest effort and outdo Ss with low motivation (Atkinson,
1958a). This corresponds to the tendency of highly motivated

persons to prefer goals of moderate probability of success, goals whose attainment depends maximally on one's own competence (cf. above, Level of Aspiration). French (1958b) has conducted an exemplary investigation of the influence of dissimilar feedback experiences. Groups of four persons each had to compose a story from given fragments. In this task they were twice interrupted briefly by the E who, for one-half of the groups, commented objectively on the success attained in working at the task, but who, for the other groups, commented sympathetically on the fine climate of cooperation. After feedback as to success of the first kind, persons with more achievement motivation than need for affiliation performed better than they did after the feedback of the second kind. Correspondingly, the reverse was true for persons with a predominant need for affiliation.

From the viewpoint of learning theory, one would speak not of feedback about success and failure but of reinforcement and extinction; or, at least, one would acknowledge a reinforcing or extinguishing function in feedback insofar as the acquisition of new behavior is concerned. Recently Burdick (1964) has made a bridge to the concept of reinforcement in learning theory and has shown that achievement motivation influences operant learning in a way for which reinforcement theory is still unprepared insofar as it is based on learning achievements of animals. In a simple stimulus discrimination experiment the S had to pull a lever if one of two visual patterns appeared; this was "rewarded" by the visible appearance of a plus sign. If the S pulled several times during the exposure of the right pattern, he received several plus signs depending on the schedule of maximum reinforcement. It was shown that, as in the case of rats and pigeons, the total frequency of all pulling responses to the correct pattern depended on the number of reinforcements that could be made during a *single* presentation of the pattern (according to E's schedule). In contrast, general accuracy of discrimination between the right and wrong patterns was not dependent on the frequency of reinforcement per single presentation but on achievement motivation. For highly motivated Ss the number of plus points accumulated for a single correct discrimination is not important. For them it is more decisive that plus points exist at all since they serve only as measures of excellence in learning as quickly and faultlessly as possible. (The effect of feedback on retrospective judgment in the postperformance period is discussed below, pp. 124 f.

III. ENDURANCE AND PERSISTENCE

Persisting at a task is a personality characteristic to a certain extent. In early childhood, one can observe a related characteristic in the performance period (Heckhausen & Roelofsen, 1962). Persistence in an induced competitive activity increases regularly between the ages of 2 and 6. Up to the age of 4½ failure produced conflict is significantly more often resolved by withdrawal and discontinuation while later on an attempt is made to overcome failure by increased effort. Winterbottom (1958) found similar correlates of enduring achievement motivation (n Achievement) in 8-year-old boys. Highly motivated Ss less often asked for help in solving puzzle tasks and declined help or rest periods offered by E more frequently than Ss with low motivation. Similar finds have been obtained for adults. Highly motivated Ss work for a much longer time than Ss with low motivation do on a complex task in which feedback about the accuracy of the proposed solutions is absent; they also perform better regardless of the time taken for the task (French & Thomas, 1958; Thomas, 1956). The prospect of finishing a task quickly and thus gaining additional free time does not constitute an incentive for highly motivated Ss in military training (French, 1955b). In a written final semester exam lasting 3 hours, highly motivated and predominantly success-motivated students turn their work in later (in other words, they work more persistently on answering the questions) than Ss with low motivation and predominant failure-motivation (Atkinson & Litwin, 1960).

Feather (1961, 1962, 1963b) has discovered that temporary situational and enduring aspects of motivation interact to influence persistence behavior. If the probability of success becomes increasingly more remote in the face of futile efforts to solve a seemingly easy task, success-motivated Ss continue their efforts for a longer time than do failure-motivated Ss. The latter shun degrees of moderate difficulty and prefer to abandon the task if it assumes this level of difficulty. In this sense, Smith (1964) was able to trace the variations in time used for a written exam back to the interaction between its experienced degree of difficulty and the level of success motivation. (Compare above, p. 96.) When achievement is "free," as with homework, failure-motivated students take longer to turn in their solutions of complex tasks; evidently they interrupt their work more often or do not engage in it for long periods (Heckhausen, 1963b). Highly motivated students are less easily dissuaded by student friends from finishing their work (Walker & Heyns, 1962). Vukovich *et al.* (1964) confirmed this uniform picture and elaborated on it out with their questionnaire results. In the face of failure and difficulties, success-motivated Ss tend to pursue a goal more persistently; however, they are not inclined toward excessive expenditure of energy. In contrast to failure-motivated Ss, they are concerned about the economy of effort. They need not compulsively fill the entire day with work (such as a highly pressured executive); rather they are able to "cut out" and enjoy "leisure time." How about study habits of college students? It is strange that this question has hardly been investigated. Although well-meaning study guides always point out that a daily work schedule is of importance, Maddox (1963) found a strict allocation of time only among students in poor standing. Able students work periodically, sometimes for 2 or 3 days without interruption; obviously they do so if "something grabs hold of them" or if "it counts." At other times they avoid work. This behavior corresponds to findings obtained for highly and success-motivated Ss.

Certain final characteristics of the performance period are worth mentioning, which, like reactive and retroactive inhibition, seem to be affected by either a high or low state of motivation. Massed practice in sensorimotor activities soon leads to a flattening of the learning curve which is usually interpreted as due to reactive inhibition or "fatigue" since it is possible to observe the phenomenon of *reminiscence* after short rest periods. That is, after the rest period, performance starts at a level higher than that attained previously. Since the strength of the reactive inhibition — as long as the person keeps working — cannot exceed the strength of motivation, after a while, the former becomes systematically related (proportional) to the latter. Thus as Kimble argued (1950), the size of the reminiscence phenomenon should reflect varying strengths of motivation after a pause of a given length during which reactive inhibition dissipates. Eysenck found such a differential reminiscence effect involving performance on the pursuit rotor task of two groups, one with little and one with strong motivation (employees and applicants for employment; Eysenck & Maxwell, 1961). McClelland and Apicella (1947) found, using a card-sorting task, that reminiscence is greater if frustration occurs before the pause, probably thus creating a failure-induced increase in the degree of motive arousal. If the pause is omitted after frustration, the improvement in performance is just as high at first, but then it falls off quickly.

It remains to be seen whether reminiscence is an ideal method for measuring motivation as Eysenck (1963) thinks. It is odd that he found the reverse effect with a cognitive activity (symbol substitution): Ss with low motivation showed a greater improvement in performance after a rest period (Eysenck & Willett, 1962). Furthermore, Miles (1958) demonstrated an *inferiority* of highly motivated Ss (IPIT scores) in relearning a sensorimotor coordination skill (again the pursuit-rotor). While they were superior to the Ss with low motivation during the original learning, they showed greater proactive inhibition during interpolated learning and greater retroactive inhibition in relearning, particularly if they were "nonanalytical" in their mode of approach (as determined by another measurement).

CHAPTER X

THE POSTPERFORMANCE PERIOD

If performance has been brought to a successful end, or to a preliminary conclusion, which exhausts present possibilities, a feeling of satisfaction ensues. As a rule, the final point has not yet been reached but rather an intermediate subgoal, a stage in the intricately worked out, achievement-oriented plan of behavior. The postperformance period is usually the occasion for apperception of subsequent activities and their organization into a time schedule.

I. RELEASE FROM THE TASK

Attention is also directed backward and surveys what was done or achieved in a critical or satisfied manner. Goal attainment is occasionally even a cause for regret or for an attempt at postponement (Henle, 1956). This has been found to be true if the activity is "purpose free," i.e. intrinsically motivated, and engaged in for its own sake rather than arriving at a fixed, final conclusion. This is the rule in playful undertakings and in solving interesting problems; it is frequently the case in risky enterprises as well as in many other, relatively "purpose-free," activities (Heckhausen, 1964b). High achievement motivation appears to promote this kind of "task-for-its-own-sake" orientation. French and Thomas (1958) have shown that highly motivated Ss, after solving a conceptual problem, persist more often in working with such problems than Ss with low motivation. This finding, however, cannot be generalized to everyday work which must be done and which does not have such explicitly "purpose-free" stimulus value. Questionnaire results show that success-motivated Ss are better able than failure-motivated Ss to quit their daily work, "cut out," and enjoy "leisure time" (Vukovich et al., 1964).

If performance ends in failure, or has to be given up as unfinished, feelings of failure result which assume different shadings and intensities according to circumstances. The result in social situations is shame: one feels "disgraced." As soon as small children are able to compete at all, they usually break off visual contact with their opponent after failure. They finger their work embarrassedly, eyes cast down, and are not able to leave the task even though they are no longer working on it (Heckhausen & Roelofsen, 1962). Helm (1954) has found this inability to quit also in college students after experiences of serious failure even though they are capable only of feeble, sporadic, and cramped efforts, and though the embarrassed behavior typical of conflict became predominant. Heckhausen and Roelofsen (1962; Heckhausen et al., 1964) and Helm have outlined the differences in the way success and failure are reacted to. After success in a social situation the psychic field is expanded, after failure it is narrowed: the almost inevitable appearance of a "cover-up" smile after failure seems to have the social function of asking for exoneration. The modes of resolution of conflict after failure have already been described and discussed (see p. 61).

Diller (1954) has traced subtle changes in self-evaluation with the aid of a method developed by Wolff (1943). In conscious self-judgments, the self is valued higher after success yet not devalued after failure. Only when the judgment is made unconsciously do negative reactions after failure occur in the self-image since they obviously cannot consciously be defended against. Wapner, Werner, and Krus (1957) have even produced changes in spatial localization. Previous experiences of success and failure affect the phenomenal level of the horizontal in a dark room. Release from a task after failure appears to be increasingly difficult the more one is bent on finishing it. At any rate, failure increases the attractiveness of tasks that one had definitely decided to finish (cf. Cohen & Zimbardo, 1962; Greenbaum *et al.*, 1965; also Cartwright, 1942, see below).

II. ZEIGARNIK EFFECT

Unfinished tasks and activities have aftereffects in the postperformance period. The best researched of these is the Zeigarnik effect (1927): unfinished activities are remembered better and longer than finished tasks and thus are recalled more easily—even spontaneously. Lewin (1926, 1946) has explained this effect with the theory of tension systems of "quasi-needs." The effect of an unfinished task on its involuntary reproduction has been uncovered most directly up to now by Fuchs (1954) with the help of the technique of conditioned activation of a motive. If the name of an unfinished task appears in the course of another task, a GSR is elicited which is followed by involuntary recall of activities involved in the first task.

In numerous subsequent investigations, the Zeigarnik effect has proved to be unstable or, more accurately, highly dependent on the situation. The effect can be obtained under ego-involving conditions (cf. Atkinson, 1953; Junker, 1960; Jäger, 1959) but as a rule it disappears (cf. Rosenzweig, 1943; Glixman, 1948; Mittag, 1955; Caron & Wallach, 1957) or is even reversed (cf. Lewis & Franklin, 1944; Smock, 1957; Green 1963). Originally, it was hypothesized that the uncompleted tasks, being failures, were suppressed. However, it is hardly possible to test such a hypothesis because it would be necessary to demonstrate first that the completed and uncompleted tasks had both been equally well learned. Such a procedure would result in new, uncontrollable rehearsal effects through the additional practice of the material required. Instead of suppression, authors such as Rosenzweig (1943) and Glixman (1948) see in the disappearance of the Zeigarnik effect under ego-involvement an ego-defense mechanism. Goldin (1964) cites characteristics of the "ego-defensive-recaller" in a summary review in which he outlines recent theoretical interpretations that depend on differences in recall that are the result of different levels of awareness.

Mittag (1955) even regards the absence of the Zeigarnik effect as a normal phenomenon since the socially mature person experiences both success and failure as belonging to the ego. However, things are not quite so simple. A study by Cartwright (1942) provides important clues to the underlying dynamic personality processes. Cartwright asked his Ss to estimate the attractiveness of a task before and after its interruption and found that valence increases after interruption for persons who speak confidently of future completion while it decreases for persons with failure expectation. This short-term change in the valence of the task is reflected in changes in the extent of motive arousal. The same external event (noncompletion of the task) results in a strengthening or weakening of motive arousal depending on the presence of either success or failure expectation (which obviously depends in good measure on the normative level of achievement motivation). Such an arousal undoubtedly influences the Zeigarnik effect decisively thereafter. Furthermore, short-term changes in motive arousal deserve closer analysis within the framework of the theory of the expectation gradient, namely, with respect to the extent to which they produce changes in the phenomenal importance of the goal, changes in its psychological attainability, or, finally, changes in both interacting on each other. (Compare Cohen & Zimbardo, 1962; Greenbaum et al., 1965.)

Cartwright's (1942) findings point to the possibility that

the disappearance of the Zeigarnik effect under ego-involvement could be the result of an experimental error (in the area of motivational psychology). Experimenters frequently present tasks which are too difficult, or allow too little time for solving them, so that one-half of the tasks will remain "uncompleted." If this creates the impression in a subject that certain tasks are too difficult, or that the time allowed is too short—so that a given task, in a borderline case, is perceived therefore as insolvable—he will not develop a level of aspiration for that task, so that it is not really "uncompleted" but rather "impossible," and thus does not represent failure.

Junker (1960) has called attention to this fact in a very careful and critical work. She has tried to clarify the ambiguous aspect of testing technique in Zeigarnik's theory: namely, whether it is the state of noncompletion or of noncorrectness of a task which is decisive for producing the effect. In one series of tests she interrupted her Ss only after incorrect performance and in another she allowed all tasks to be completed, but half of them incorrectly. Her results confirmed the fact that it is the need for the correctness and not for completion of an activity that leads to better recall, to the Zeigarnik effect, regardless of whether the tasks were executed in an examination situation or to please the E. Marrow (1938) had already shown earlier that completion in itself is not decisive. He reversed the test technique: if the S is on the path to the right solution he is interrupted by the E; if the E allows the task to be completed, this is an indication for the S that he has *not* solved it successfully. The "completed" (failed) tasks are remembered better under these conditions. Accordingly, it is success and failure, and not (external) completion or interruption, which are decisive in producing the Zeigarnik effect.

Jäger (1959) also found the Zeigarnik effect among Ss who were exposed to a really serious examination which was instrumental in their professional promotion. However, he found it only when recall took place shortly after the examination (30 minutes later). Just one day later the Zeigarnik effect was reversed, and 2 and 6–9 days later successfully completed material was remembered significantly better. Jäger explains this result by arguing that as time passed after the examination the task material lost importance in the memory traces, and personality mechanisms, such as the need to defend against failure, took over. It remains to be considered, of course, whether the valence of the failed material changes as time passes, for the growing lapse of time increases the certainty that the unsatisfactorily solved problems on the examination cannot be made up and that they represent the final result which has to be accepted.

To summarize, it can be stated that the real conditions governing the appearance of the Zeigarnik effect have not been completely clarified to date. However, this has not prevented several authors from using it as a validation criterion for various theoretical formulations. Butterfield (1964) discusses this problem in a summary review.

Effects of personality factors have been isolated in many studies. The following enumeration presents a selection of personality traits (achievement motivation excepted) which correlate with the *absence* of the Zeigarnik effect: "ego strength" (Alper, 1946, 1952; Eriksen, 1954); "realistic self-esteem" (Coopersmith, 1960); "striving for prestige" (Mittag, 1955); "low perseverance for achievement" (Caron & Wallach, 1959); "nonvolunteering" for participation in a test (Green, 1963). As diverse as the picture appears, all the investigations, despite widely varying test conditions agree that the absence of the Zeigarnik effect can best be explained by taking into consideration the interaction between the present situation and enduring personality traits. Such a result, however, is so general that it is valid for all findings in the psychology of motivation.

What has the concept of achievement motivation contributed to the clarification of the effect? According to Atkinson's findings (1953; Atkinson & Raphelson, 1956; Moulton, 1958; also Caron & Wallach, 1959, with a different motivational measure), the recall of unfinished tasks increases as a function of the strength of achievement motivation to the extent to which the situation permits no doubt that noncompletion means failure. The difference in recall may be explained as an instrumental act in the postperformance period. The recall of unsolved tasks is thus in the service of increased motivation, namely, to achieve success even with them. On the other hand, the recall of solved tasks is in the service of failure avoidance (moderate strength of motivation) since the memory of failures is avoided. [Compare, however, a somewhat reversed interpretation by Alper (1957) in terms of her strong and weak ego dimension.] The hypothesized process of avoidance has found a certain confirmation in the differing recall of success and failure stories which Reitman (1961) found to be a joint function of enduring motivational level and of situational arousal. Predominantly failure-motivated persons (middle third of the n Achievement distribution) "forget" more of the failure stories under achievement-related arousal even though they were able to reproduce them better than nonfailure motivated persons under neutral conditions.

Some findings of Heckhausen (1963b) may be interpreted in the same way. He found that failure-motivated Ss recall more solved tasks than success-motivated Ss (and, on the whole, remember more tasks in general). The corresponding reversal for unsolved tasks, however, was not found; these were recalled equally well by both groups. In contrast to Atkinson, the Zeigarnik effect was more pronounced the *lower* the total motivation. This seems to agree with the frequent observation that better recall of unsolved tasks disappears with a rising level of motive arousal ("ego involvement") (cf. Green, 1963).

A reconciliation of Atkinson's and Heckhausen's contradictory findings (although obtained under divergent conditions) is still to be made. The separation of situational and enduring motivational factors was inadequate in both studies. Götzl's (1960, in Heckhausen, 1963b) experiment, based on a method Ferdinand developed (1959), yielded a result which shows a certain similarity with the correlation between the Zeigarnik effect and success motivation. Success-motivated persons, compared to failure-motivated persons, remembered more tasks during the postperformance period when the results were made known in 8 weeks rather than in 2 days. Thus, the success-motivated Ss included both types of tasks in a comprehensive time span developed in the postperformance period.

Finally, a kind of aftereffect of noncompletion, other than recall, should be mentioned, namely, *resumption* of tasks (cf. Ovsiankina, 1928). Coopersmith (1960) offered 11- to 12-year-old pupils each a previously solved and an unsolved task to work on again. The more pronounced the success-oriented achievement motivation (positive categories of the n Achievement measure), the more frequently the unsolved task is resumed.

Apparently the reverse was found by Weiner (1965a), but he interpolated success or failure experiences on another activity before the original tasks could be resumed. Immediately after success experiences, more low n Achievement ("failure-motivated") than high n Achievement Ss tended to resume interrupted tasks. A tentative explanation may be given along the lines of N. E. Miller's (1944) conflict model (cf. p. 56).

If these findings are added to those with the Zeigarnik effect, it can be concluded in summary that the tendency to complete something uncompleted quickly increases with increasing strength of success-oriented achievement motivation (cf. Section III, Endurance and Persistence, in Chapter IX).

III. RETROSPECTIVE JUDGMENT OF SUCCESS

Retrospective judgment of what has been attained is no less

influenced by motivational factors. In the case of 6- to 7-year-old children, attained success still appears to be generally salient. As reported by Mehl (1962, p. 200) the number of winnings (obtained objectively by chance, yet experienced as dependent upon achievement) is guessed more accurately than the number of losses by both winners and losers. Nuttin (1953) presented older pupils and adults with a series of twenty size-estimation tasks of the same kind and after each solution, he passed it off as wrong or right (there were always ten right and ten wrong ones). A group of "pessimists" ("living in an atmosphere of failure"), as determined by the judgment of others, overestimated the number of failures, and a group of "optimists" overestimated the number of successes. Nuttin explains this assimilation effect with the need of the ego for internal consistency (*besoin de consistance interne*).

Using the same method Heckhausen (1958, 1963b) found a marked inverse relationship between such probability estimates and achievement motivation and, what is more remarkable, it appeared only after an achievement frame of reference had been established by twice-repeating the size-estimation tasks. Under conditions of strong reality constraint, namely with immediate and unequivocal feedback about success and failure, success-motivated persons *overestimated their failures* and failure-motivated persons their successes. This inverse relationship can best be understood as an effect of the frame of reference: experiences which do not coincide with the expectations based on enduring motivational level (normative state) contrast more strongly with background expectations. On the other hand, if unequivocal information about the results of a performance attempt is omitted, the inverse relationship between motivation and judgment is reversed into a positive relationship. With weak reality constraints, it is possible that situations which do not clearly correspond to, or which *appear* to contradict expectations, are redefined into what is expected or feared, that is, are changed and adapted to what is expected.

CHAPTER XI

ACCOMPLISHMENTS

This chapter is meant to cover the many ways in which achievement-related actions can be evaluated as "well done." The influence of motivation on accomplishment is less direct than is generally assumed at first. Potential motivation is only one factor among many that interact complexly to produce an accomplishment (cf. Heckhausen, 1963b, p. 269 ff.). To begin with, potential motivation has to be aroused by situational cues (cf. above: Valence and Motive Arousal). Then other factors come into play. The actual ability to function is determined by various factors: first, by talent and acquired abilities, then by special styles of functioning (as in the so-called "cognitive styles"). In addition, there are temporary states of functioning behavioral systems, such as fatigue, sensory deprivation, and social isolation (cf. Suedfeld, Grissom, & Vernon, 1964). A decisive role is played by the height of the activation level. The relative importance of all those factors finally depends on the nature of the task.

Since we have already discussed the interaction of various determinants of behavior, such as apperception and activation, in what follows we will merely describe relationships between motivation and accomplishment rather than try to analyze them in terms of the ways in which they might come to be related. We will concentrate on the connections of motivation with intelligence, with success in school and college, and on tasks which place various demands on the individual.

(Findings concerning persistence and success in the recall of completed and uncompleted tasks will not be dealt with further.)

I. MOTIVATION AND INTELLIGENCE

The relationships between motivation and intelligence have not as yet been systematically investigated. This is strange but not surprising inasmuch as theory has hardly built any bridges between the two areas of research. Present results are incidental findings. As a rule they do not reveal statistically significant correlations between achievement motivation and intelligence test scores (McClelland *et al.*, 1953, p. 274; French, 1955a; Krumboltz & Farquhar, 1957; McClelland, 1958a; Weiss, Wertheimer, & Groesbeck, 1959; Mahone, 1960; Hayashi, Okamoto, & Habu, 1962; Bartmann, 1963; Caron, 1963; Vukovich *et al.*, 1964; Smith, 1964). It would be premature to conclude, however, in the absence of theoretical treatment, that the two variables are functionally unrelated (or that there is no validity in the motivation measure since a relation to accomplishment cannot be obtained; cf. Krumboltz, 1957; Krumboltz & Farquhar, 1957). Different kinds of relationships may be obscured in the total sample and may appear only if one discovers the selection criteria necessary to produce homogeneous subsamples. Occasionally it has been supposed that the same intelligence test performance can be produced by mutually compensating contributions from intelligence and motivation. Such a complementary relationship ought to result in a negative correlation between the two variables if the group of Ss is homogeneous in the sense that they all have reached the same performance level. It is not surprising that such negative correlations have not been reported since the complementarity of intelligence and motivation could show up only under very narrowly defined conditions.

In contrast to the complementarity model, there is undoubtedly an upper limit in distribution of intelligence from which point on accomplishments (which also include intelligence test scores) depend decisively on differences in motivation (cf. McClelland *et al.*, 1958a, p. 13); there is also a lower limit at which point motivation becomes irrelevant. More precisely: from a certain high degree of native ability on up, improvements in intelligent performances is promoted more by increases in the strength of motivation than by increases in the level of native capacity which is already high; and conversely below a certain low level of native capacity, improvements in intelligent performances are favored more by increases in the low level of native capacity than by increases in the strength of motivation. Confining the experimental samples of Ss to the upper end of the intelligence distribution, therefore, ought to uncover closer connections of accomplishment with motivation (paradoxically, i.e., contrary to the usual finding that a wide range generally produces a higher correlation).

This seems indeed to be the case. Such restricted samples have been drawn in at least three of the five investigations which have found a positive relationship between achievement motivation and level of intelligence. French and Thomas (1958) worked with Air Force recruits with intelligence test scores in the upper 11% of the distribution, and from these they chose only the highly motivated. They found a correlation of .36 between achievement motivation and intelligence. Robinson (1961, 1964) obtained a correlation of .40 for a group of 11- and 12-year-old children in the upper half of the intelligence distribution. Meyer *et al.* (1965) found close connections between achievement motivation (AM) and intelligence (on Thurstone's Primary Mental Abilities Test) in the third grade if the sample was restricted to the best pupils in class from several large cities, i.e., to those having an IQ of over 105. Intelligence test scores correlated .52 with success moti-

vation, and .50 with total motivation (HS + FF). Similar correlations have been reported by McClelland *et al.* (1953, p. 235,
237) for college war veterans and college students.

The samples in the latter instances are perhaps less homogeneous with respect to high intelligence than with respect
to sociological group membership. The latter, combined with
the former, is important for another theory of the connection
between intelligence and motivation. It is more enlightening
to conceive of the two as *interacting in combination* rather
than as complementary: greater capacity favors the intensification of achievement motivation, and high achievement motivation contributes to the expression or use of capacity. This
has already been demonstrated. According to French (1958a),
excellence of performance in a complex task correlates with
level of intelligence only in the case of highly motivated
Ss. One may therefore assume that motivation existed to
make full use of capacity. Findings in the longitudinal investigations by Kagan, Sontag, Baker, and Nelson (1958) and
Kagan and Moss (1959) are even more revealing. Between
the ages of 6 and 15, the IQ (Stanford-Binet) of highly motivated children kept rising while it remained the same or decreased for children with low motivation. Again, the test
sample was socioeconomically rather restricted (middle-class)
from the upper intelligence range (mean IQ = 120).

This is important since if capacity and motivation are to
influence each other a mediating link is required, namely,
reinforcement for accomplishment. This can occur regularly
only within the confines of a restricted sociological group,
which is homogenous in regard to defined standards of excellence, thus mediating the interaction between capacity
and motivation; different social classes (and their subcultures)
provide different types and amounts of reinforcement for
performance which depends on the kind and degree of intelligence demanded. Thus, for instance, in a lower social class
performance of an absolute lower capacity level may be

linked to the same amount of reinforcement for accomplishment (and, by interaction, to the same strength of motivation) which, in a middle class group, requires accomplishments of a higher or more complex level. The varying quality and length of education in the different social classes is an outstanding indicator of the reinforcement provided for achievement. However, higher educational demands are met in the higher social classes not only by a rise in the average intelligence level. Achievement motivation also generally increases from lower to higher social classes and middle class males (Class II) generally have the highest scores (Rosen, 1956, 1961; Nuttall, 1964) even if education is used as criterion of membership in a social class (Veroff *et al.*, 1960; Littig & Yeracaris, 1963; Nuttall, 1964). Whatever the connection may be in an individual, the relationship between intelligence and motivation would be further clarified if samples were restricted to those which are homogeneous with respect to the linkage of standards of excellence to amount of achievement reinforcement provided in the life space of a social class.

II. ACHIEVEMENT IN SCHOOL AND COLLEGE

One ought also to consider the mediating dimension of reinforcement for accomplishment when he seeks the connection between motivation and achievement in school, college, or career. This question is less "academic" than the one dealing with the interactions of motivation and intelligence. It is of great practical importance to be able to predict the future achievement of individuals. A great many investigations have been carried out on this point.[11] Most of these

---

[11] We need not consider research results with motivational measures based on questionnaires which are frequently used for the prediction of educational or professional achievement, such as the

report relations between high, or success-related, motivation and educational accomplishment. This is not surprising since the functional relationship is more direct than can exist for the interactions of much longer duration between motivation and intelligence. Highly motivated pupils and college students do better in school and in college (McClelland *et al.*, 1953, p. 237 and 240; Rosen, 1956; Weiss *et al.*, 1959; Shaw, 1961; Uhlinger & Stephens, .1960; Robinson, 1964; Meyer *et al.*, 1965). Four studies demonstrated this for success in the study of psychology alone (McKeachie *et al.*, 1955; Atkinson & Litwin, 1960; McKeachie, 1961; Heckhausen, 1963b; however, Bendig, 1958, 1959, did not verify the finding). The relationship holds not only for high achievement motivation but also for predominantly success-oriented achievement motivation (Heckhausen, 1963b; Meyer *et al.*, 1965) and for a combination of high *n* Achievement and low test anxiety (TAQ; Atkinson & Litwin, 1960). As had to be expected, the correlations are moderate and rarely go above $r = .40$.

The picture hardly changes if the possible effects of differences in intelligence are eliminated by sample selection (Morgan, 1952; Uhlinger & Stephens, 1960) or by partialling them out statistically (McClelland *et al.*, 1953, p. 237; Ricciuti & Sadacca, 1955). Intelligence measures, obviously, contribute significantly to the improvement of accuracy in the prediction of achievement in school and college based on motivation scores. Weiss *et al.* (1959) were able to raise the coefficient of $r = .34$ based on motivation alone to $R = +.63$ after inclusion of scores on the "Academic Aptitude Test." Stanford, Dember, and Stanford (1963) were able to raise the Chi^2 values of 2.08 for achievement anxiety (AAT) and of

scales of the "Edwards Personal Preference Schedule" (EPPS, A. L. Edwards, 1954) or the "California Personality Inventory (CPI, Gough, 1957, 1964). EPPS *n* Achievement and TAT *n* Achievement do not correlate (cf. Melikian, 1958; Marlowe, 1959; Atkinson & Litwin, 1960).

11.44 for IQ to 25.84 when they considered both criteria together as predictors of school achievement. Dember *et al.* (1962) obtained prediction coefficients of over .60 with a combination of AAT and a school qualification test (cf. Milholland, 1964).

Lowell (in McClelland *et al.*, 1953, p. 238), Mitchell (1961), and Caron (1963) found no relation between motivation and academic achievement; neither did Hayashi *et al.* (1962) and Cole, Jacobs, Zubok, Fagot, and Hunter (1962) who, however, drew their samples from widely divergent groups so that the absence of a relation is not surprising for the reasons discussed above. To date, few results have been reported on the relation of occupational success to achievement motivation. In general n Achievement has shown no relation to creativity in the physical sciences (McClelland *et al.*, 1953, and McClelland, 1964d); on the other hand, it is related to business success (McClelland, 1961, 1965a,b), particularly in the sales area (Litwin, 1964). The proper selection of measures and samples sets some difficult problems. McClelland (1961) has discussed this in part in the case of entrepreneurial success in the economy. He was able to show in a mechanical skills training program in India that success in starting small enterprises correlated with achievement motivation measured a year or so earlier.

III. OTHER TYPES OF ACCOMPLISHMENT

Relationships have been found between achievement motivation and a variety of more narrowly defined accomplishments than success in school. In what follows we will group the results according to the nature of the demands set by various tasks. In general, Ss with higher achievement motivation (especially if they are success-oriented rather than failure-oriented) do better on all sorts of tasks; this is true particularly of tasks which permit learning, demand concentration, or contain levels of difficulty which by mastering one's competence can be demonstrated.

This is the case, for example, for tasks of an intricate variety such as were presented to Ss by French and Thomas (1958) and French (1958a). Bartmann (1965) has shown that success-motivated persons (HS-FF, AM) enter more deeply (cf. p. 139) into *conceptual problems* of the Katona (1940) and Wertheimer (1957) type which require insight. After a period of *programmed instruction,* they show a greater improvement in performance, the correlation being independent of intelligence. Success-motivated Ss are superior in tasks requiring quick perception and practical reasoning (such as technical construction problems and coin-sorting) if the situation is made more achievement-oriented by mild time pressure (Bartmann, 1963). In "water pitcher problems," of the Luchins type (1942), highly and success-motivated Ss display less rigidity of thought (R. W. Brown, 1953; Atkinson & Raphelson, 1956; not, however, French, 1955a). After a brief period of exposure to a difficult passage on psychological theory, success-motivated pupils (of equal intelligence) obtained a better understanding of it as demonstrated by their use of it in understanding similar problems; however, they were not superior in the reproduction of particular details (Caron, 1963; cf. above, p. 73).

Highly motivated Ss also do better on tasks requiring *language ability* or skills, such as anagrams (formation of new words from a given combination of letters, McClelland *et al.,* 1953; Clark & McClelland, 1956), *scrambled word tests* (Lowell, 1952; French & Lesser, 1964), composition of stories from given sentences (French, 1958b), *production of ideas* on problems relating to their preferred value orientation ("the female role among women undergraduates," French & Lesser, 1964). Their *verbal fluency* appears to be greater (Wagner & Williams, 1961, using IPIT).

They are also superior in some *verbal memory tasks.* They

are quicker in learning pairs of nonsense syllables (Sampson, 1963) and recall more unusual details of intelligible material (a short story) when there was no intent to learn (Karolchuck & Worell, 1956). They remember success and failure-related material equally well while failure-motivated Ss remember failure material better under neutral conditions and success material better under achievement-oriented conditions (Reitman, 1961). Failure-motivated Ss, compared to the others, are able to recall more on a short-term basis under intent to learn; highly motivated Ss, on the other hand, recall more when they are unexpectedly allowed to reproduce stories which they themselves have composed 9 days earlier (DeCharms *et al.*, 1955). When immediate recall is involved, they reproduce verbal passages more literally (Lazarus *et al.*, 1957). They are faster in simple coding tasks (French, 1955b; Birney, 1958b). Angelini (1959) reports high correlation of *n* Achievement with three learning tasks which are not described in detail.

Among *tasks requiring perception,* maze learning should be mentioned first. Highly motivated Ss learn more quickly and work with fewer errors (Johnston, 1955, using IPIT; Heckhausen, 1963b; Bartmann, 1963). They make more progress in a course designed to improve reading speed (Botha & Close, 1964). They are quicker in learning skills requiring sensorimotor coordination; however, they take longer in unlearning them (pursuit meter; Miles, 1958, using IPIT). According to Ryan and Lakie (1965) they show greater gains in performance in going from a relaxed to a competitive situation, particularly if they are success-motivated (high in FTI, low in MAS). In simple *speed* tests as in marking circles with crosses as fast as possible, their quantitative achievement is greater only if this activity has explicitly been represented as relevant to achievement (Atkinson & Raphelson, 1956), or if there is a prospect of reward (Murstein & Collier, 1962). Atkinson and Reitman (1956) were not able to confirm this result but probably only because of a simultaneously presented memory test to which the highly motivated Ss appeared to pay more attention. No difference was found for a *checking* task involving digit symbol substitution (Reitman, 1960). Miller and Worchel (1956) also obtained negative results, as did Vogel *et al.* (1958), with a checking task in which varying combinations of three symbols had to be noted and counted. In both cases, however, the checking task was executed under extreme failure-inducing conditions. Vogel *et al.* (1958) even found higher quantitative achievement under these conditions for Ss with low motivation and for "underachievers" (pupils with school performance below their native ability). The number of Rorschach responses, which has been used as indicator of "ambition to produce quantity," does not increase among highly motivated Ss but rather among failure-motivated persons (McClelland *et al.*, 1953).

Cognitive style in perception (as measured by "Embedded Figures" tests, "Figure Completion" tests, and others) correlates with achievement motivation. Highly motivated persons are more "field-independent"; in other words, they proceed more flexibly and more analytically as French (1955a) and Wertheim and Mednick (1958) were able to demonstrate with adults; Honigfeld and Spigel (1960) showed this only for women, not men, and Crandall and Sinkeldam (1964) for 6- to 12-year-old children. Meyer *et al.* (1965) report a relationship between field dependency and failure motivation in 9- to 11-year-old pupils. Reitman (1960) did not find any difference in the ability to *recognize transposed shapes.* Highly motivated Ss learn simple discriminations of visual designs more quickly and faultlessly (Burdick, 1964).

Recognition thresholds for relevant content seem to be influenced by various evaluative dispositions relating to achievement motivation. Highly motivated Ss have, under achievement-oriented arousal, lower thresholds for success and failure words than have Ss with low motivation (Moulton *et al.*, 1958), particularly for success words, while the highest thresholds are found among failure-motivated persons for failure words (McClelland & Liberman, 1949). Highly motivated Ss have less accurate *interpersonal sensitivity* in the achievement area (Berlew & Williams, 1964). Finally, even *autokinetic movement* must be mentioned. In highly motivated Ss it moves less to the right—a fact which Fisher (1961) attempts to explain via a long-standing relationship between ability to postpone gratification and distribution of tonus on the two sides of the body. That is, postponement of gratification, which is characteristic of highly motivated Ss normally takes place via actions involving the right side of the body.

A popular measure of achievement is provided by *mental arithmetic problems* which require the execution of several part operations and the short-term recollection of intermediate results. Performance correlates with individual arithmetic skill (Reitman, 1960), but not with "intelligence" in the sense of deductive thinking (Spitzer, 1961) Mental arithmetic is so "overlearned" among older pupils and college students that progress in learning during an experiment cannot be observed. In contrast to most of the above-mentioned measures, this measure of accomplishment is, therefore, independent of learning and is essentially a reflection of the concentration and effort expended on mental operations. Therefore, highly motivated persons have proved throughout to be superior in such a task, although their arithmetic skill is not greater than that of Ss with low motivation (Lowell, 1952; Atkinson & Reitman, 1956). This has been shown repeatedly for the addition of three two-digit figures (Lowell, 1952; Birney, 1958b) and for the well-known Düker tasks (1949) both with regard to the quantity and quality of arithmetic performance (Wendt, 1955; Atkinson & Reitman, 1956; Reitman & Atkinson, 1958; Klauer, 1961). Experiments involving group competition and experimentally manipulated prospects of success have shown that highly motivated Ss do better only if the number of winners is fixed at less than half of the group (Atkinson, 1958a; McClelland, 1961, p. 218).

It is noteworthy that the closest relationships between motivation and achievement are obtained when the situation is achievement-oriented and the pace of work is left open (Wendt, 1955, and Klauer, 1961, as well as in a personal communication, report $r = .49$ and $r = .45$, respectively). If the Ss are forced by E (Wendt, 1955), or required to adhere to a required rate of work, performance improves (Düker, 1931) although the relationship with differences in motivation disappears. They evidently no longer make a difference because situational pressure has pushed performance up to its ceiling. Tent (1963) did find a superiority among more highly motivated Ss (based on a questionnaire measure) on a task requiring Ss to put out their maximum effort for 3 hours! Contrary to expectation, a complex experimental design by Reitman (1960) and investigations by Murstein and Collier (1962) and Murstein (1963) did not yield positive correlations. (The last two investigations, however, were affected by an experimental error resulting from inappropriate conditions for n Achievement arousal.) Highly motivated Ss (Williams, 1955, using IPIT) also work faster on simpler tasks involving addition and subtraction of three one-digit numbers.

Finally, the least demand on the S is made by a task requiring addition of pairs of one-digit figures. For such a task Heckhausen (1963b) found that performance correlates not with the strength but with the direction of motivation: failure-motivated Ss work faster than success-motivated Ss and are able to maintain the level of their initial performance for a longer period. The greater exertion of the former can probably be traced to the stronger incentive which this trivial and thus harmless (with regard to possible failure) task provides for failure-motivated Ss. Vogel *et al.* (1958) explain the superiority of college students with low motivation on a simple task of speed in this way. A similar explanation may account for the greater number of responses in the Rorschach test produced by failure-motivated Ss (McClelland *et al.,* 1953). Activities which can be failed rarely or not at all and, therefore, do not open up any possibilities for the test of one's competence, obviously leave highly and success-motivated Ss "cold" unless the E represents the task as particularly informative about personal competence. Atkinson and Raphelson (1956) apparently were able to create such an impression for a task involving the rapid marking of circles with crosses, whereas Atkinson and Reitman (1956) were not able to.

Since we have already discussed the matter above and in other connections, we would like to refer only briefly in conclusion to factors affecting the relationship between potential achievement motivation and final accomplishment. The valence of a task (i.e., its attractiveness) is affected, as already noted, by success or failure motivation. The "motive arousal content" of the total situation is also of decisive importance. For instance, if the degree of probability of future failure can no longer be controlled, failure-motivated Ss leave the field psychologically; they "cut out" (Raphelson & Moulton, 1958). A relaxation of situational pressure, however, may improve their ability to achieve even under prospects of failure (Mc-Keachie, Pollie, & Speisman, 1955). Situational stress, such as mild time pressure inducement, is detrimental to failure-motivated Ss and beneficial to success-motivated Ss (Bartmann, 1963). A strict, achievement-oriented college course paralyzes initiative and efficiency in highly motivated students while it evokes more effort from students with low motivation (McKeachie, 1961). Success-motivated Ss profit more if, on the other hand, the individual can set his own working pace in a programmed course of instruction with teaching machines (Bartmann, 1965).

The examples could be multiplied. Future research will have to control experimental conditions better and in a greater variety of ways in order to differentiate the sometimes beneficial and sometimes detrimental effects of situational stress (cf. the former summary review by Lazarus, Deese, & Osler, 1952).[12] After one has measured stable motivational levels, he should also obtain individual differences in the arousal value of the situation and in the level of activation; and of course native ability factors also ought to be controlled. What is more, the effect of all these variables depends in the end on the demands of the task. Thus, achievement in simple sensorimotor tasks of speed improves with increasing situational pressure and increasing levels of activation, while it declines under the same conditions for more complex cognitive tasks, once a certain level of complexity has been passed (e.g., Vogel *et al.*, 1959; Hebb, 1955; Duffy, 1957).

---

[12] Highly relevant is Weiner's recent study (1966) on the role of success and failure in the learning of easy and complex tasks. The results are contradictory to predictions from Spence's drive theory (1958).

CHAPTER XII

ORIGIN AND DEVELOPMENT OF ACHIEVEMENT MOTIVATION

Only recently have researchers begun to look for a pervasive achievement-related motivational characteristic in the development of children's accomplishments as they have been recorded in great numbers by classical developmental psychology. White (1959, 1960) has impressively explicated how a child's development is furthered by "effectance motivation": by the drive to deal with the environment, to influence it actively, and thus to experience, to expand, and to maximize (McCall, 1963) his own effectiveness and competence (cf. Woodworth, 1958). Paradoxically, the obviousness of these phenomena seems to be the reason for their belated consideration because the powerful fascination of psychoanalytic theory has led more and more to the conviction that really important motives ought to be very much hidden in early childhood.

I. PRECURSORS AND FIRST APPEARANCE

Phenomena which appear to be "achievement motivated" in early childhood include various behavior repetitions which Bühler (1919) interpreted as "function pleasure" ("Funktionslust") and Piaget (1936) as circular reactions; particularly "wanting-to-do-it-alone" (Fales, in Lewin *et al.*, 1944; Müller,

1958; Klamma, 1957) can be observed at the start of the second year during familiar routines in the home, such as during eating or dressing. These modes of behavior seem to be more basic than acquired because each child abandons himself to the task with concentration, persistence, and satisfaction and yet does not need positive reinforcement from the parents, which he usually does not get anyway, and he frequently persists in his behavior despite negative sanctions. It is noteworthy that the early demand of a child that he do something by himself is made only for those activities the mastery of which has just been acquired, or acquired not long ago, and that the demand is given up if still greater difficulties have to be overcome.

The independence with which routine skills once acquired are practiced has no connection with the achievement-related behavior characteristic of self-reliance (Beller, 1957; Winterbottom, 1958; Heckhausen & Kemmler, 1957). The most impressive type of "achievement behavior" during the first 3 years of life is the persistence in sensorimotor activities involving objects (for instance, in erecting things, stringing pearls, painting). Kagan and Moss (1962), however, found that the duration of being occupied with something in early childhood had no predictive value for the salience of later achievement behavior; in contrast, more intellectual activities, such as talking and counting, during the subsequent "conceptual" stage (Piaget, 1936) did have predictive value.

It is, therefore, improbable that there is continuity in the development of achievement motivation before the age of 3, although one has to be prepared in principle to find complex relationships with happenings in earliest childhood. Wendt (1961) has at least made it seem probable that the origin of risk-taking behaviors occurs at the time of first sitting-up and learning-to-walk which are "sensitive periods" during which the relatively unpredictable behavior of the mother appears to "imprint" the child in ways which are expressed as risk-taking preferences in adolescents and adults. It is noteworthy that the preverbal stage of sitting-up has an "imprinting" effect only if it coincides with the rise and fall in the mother's general activity level at different times of the year. He has not obtained relationships with achievement motivation.

Heckhausen and his collaborators (1962, 1964, 1965) consider the aforementioned phenomena of "function pleasure," of wanting-to-do-it-alone, and of persistence in sensorimotor activities to be precursors, but not the beginnings, of achievement motivation in the narrower sense. Achievement motivation presupposes the structuring of the situation within an achievement-related person-environment frame of reference, of which children first become capable between the ages of 3 and 3½ —in other words, at a time when "the success or failure of one's activity directs the pleasure or disappointment no longer only at the outcome of the activity as such but rather at the self, so that with success the child experiences pleasure about his competence, and with failure experiences shame about his incompetence" (Heckhausen & Roelofsen, 1962, p. 378; cf. Bialer, 1961, and the descriptive system in Heckhausen & Wagner, 1965).

The origin of a motive, therefore, lies neither in the appearance of something laid down innately nor in the descent from ontogenetically earlier motives, as has been vaguely assumed by Crandall, Preston and Rabson (1960b, p. 788). Rather it appears along with the cognitive step in maturing which enables the above-mentioned structuring of the person-environment frame of reference to take place. As a rule, this step is not taken before the age of 3 as has been confirmed by other research on competition among small children of that age (Greenberg, 1932; Leuba, 1933; McKee & Leader, 1955). In a comparison of the behavior of 3- and of 4-year-old children after failure in an activity, Zunich (1964) observed that the

4-year-olds show stronger reactions to failure; they no longer give up easily, and ask an adult for help more rarely than 3-year olds do.

That the first appearance of achievement motivation has to do with a cognitive and not any other developmental condition has been shown by research on competitive behavior among imbeciles (Heckhausen & Wasna, 1965). All the signs of achievement-motivated behavior can also be found in the feeble-minded, independent of age (contrary to generalizations by Hoppe, 1932, and Gottschaldt, 1933), as long as mental development is above the stage of 3½ years and as long as the cognitive demands of the task do not surpass the level of mental development attained. From their onset, success and failure[13] are experienced vividly. They can be recognized in contrary types of expressive behavior (Heckhausen & Roelofsen, 1962; Heckhausen, Ertel, & Kiekheben-Roelofsen, 1964). The intensity of failure experience is noteworthy. The conflict thus occasioned between desire for success and fear of failure leads above all in little children (up to the age of 4½) to trying out an inventive repertoire of inadequate solution attempts which, in its basic structure, already includes everything that can be isolated in adults. Thus, failure, instead of being admitted and overcome, is denied, concealed, excused, or carefully evaded, either by avoiding a renewed effort at achievement or by precluding the possibility of failure by taking elaborate precautions (cf. above, Resolution of Conflict after Failure, p. 61).

The origin of the capacity for conflict between the desire for achievement and the prospect of failure obviously depends on the relative prominence of the given prospects for

[13] Success and failure here should always be understood in the achievement-related sense only. Something entirely different is meant by Fajans (1933) when she uses the terms to cover gratification or frustration of the need to grasp, possess, or eat, which she found to be present even in infants.

success or failure. If the probabilities of success and failure are equal, children up to 4½ years of age remain completely confident in their expectation of success; equal probabilities are evaluated realistically, and may therefore cause conflict, only from the age of 4½ on (Heckhausen & Roelofsen, 1962). On the other hand, children from 3½ years of age on have been shown to be capable of conflict if they have to choose among tasks of increasing degrees of difficulty and if they have to consider tasks at which they will probably fail. It is noteworthy, however, that they are capable of a real decision only after the age of 4½, that is, in the sense that the decision frees them from the conflict; they also begin at this age to show intraindividual consistency in the preference for a certain level of difficulty in goal setting (Heckhausen & Wagner, 1965). The origin of level of aspiration (in the sense of calculated goal setting to maximize gains), therefore, comes about 1 year after the origin of achievement motivation.

Thus, within 1 year (from the age of 4½ on) individual levels of achievement motivation can be clearly recognized. This has also been confirmed by individual preferences for levels of difficulty in a ring-tossing game observed by Mc-Clelland (1958a) in 5-year-old children. Müller (1958) noted the formation of a level of aspiration, beginning at age 5, for a task in which excellence was measured by the time needed for its execution. Three- and four-year-old children are obviously cognitively overtaxed by such tasks inasmuch as Müller was not able to establish in them the experiences of success, failure, or conflict. More suitable are tasks in which the levels of difficulty can be seen. Thus, Anderson (in Lewin *et al.*, 1944) used ring-tossing from different distances and found that the maturity of rules-of-the-game behavior so far as it concerns level of aspiration increases between the ages of 3 and 5½ and is practically perfect by the age of 8. According to McClelland (1958a) this is apparently true for 5-year-old children, too, since their preferred levels of difficulty in a ring-tossing game correlate with their achievement motivation to an extent that is found also in adults (cf. p. 93). Sears and Levin (1957) had 4- and 5-year-olds choose different heavy weights for lifting (and similar things); however, they merely found that the children were more cautious and chose lower goals when they were given a second trial after some days.

II. GENERAL COURSE OF DEVELOPMENT

Concentration and persistence in the pursuit of achievement goals increase with age, clearly from 4½ years on, and failures are tolerated better and more frequent attempts are made to overcome them (Heckhausen and collaborators, 1962, 1965). Rosenzweig (1933, 1945) and Bialer (1961) observed the tendency to overcome failure over a period from 4–14 years of age. When faced with a choice between tasks which had been successfully solved or failed, the older ones increasingly preferred to resume the unsolved task. This tendency is connected with high and success-oriented achievement motivation as Coopersmith (1960) was able to show for 11- to 12-year-olds.

Crandall and Rabson (1960) found a sex difference. After entering school, girls continued to prefer to work with solved tasks while boys attempted to master the ones which they had failed. In the case of 3- and 4-year-olds, according to Zunich (1964), girls attempted to overcome failure in a more independent and persistent way while boys reacted rather in an affective and inadequate way. (Heckhausen and collaborators, 1962, 1965, on the other hand, did not find any sex differences between the age of 2 and 6). During the course of growing up boys are obviously faced more strongly than girls with the necessity to master fear of failure and (as, for instance, in the choice of a career) not to evade the problem of achievement (cf. Barry, Bacon, & Child, 1957; Johnson, 1963). Thus, only in women does the fear of, and tendency to evade, failure, observed in childhood, correlate with interview data relating to the same tendencies in adulthood (Kagan & Moss, 1962).

Detailed longitudinal studies for four age periods from 0 to 14 years and into adulthood have been undertaken at the Fels Research Institute. Various aspects of achievement-related behavior were judged by observation of a child and from statements of an adult in an interview. As reported by Kagan and Moss (1962), a remarkable stability exists from the age of 3 into adulthood for individual levels of achievement behavior (especially in the intellectual area) and for the disposition toward competition. Striving for achievement-related recognition and fear of failure were noted from the age of 6. Also, achievement motivation measured by the TAT method (n Achievement) shows moderate but significant stability between the ages 8 and 11 and between the ages of 14 and 25. For age periods 14 and 25 (but not age periods 8 and 11) it correlates with achievement performances at the same age periods.

Beginning at age 3, more so at 6, and most at 10, intelligence is also related to the various types of achievement-motivated behavior shown in childhood and adulthood; it is not only the absolute height of the IQ which is so related to achievement motivation but, significantly enough, also its relative increase between the ages of 6 and 10 which, furthermore, is accompanied by stronger achievement motivation in the TAT (Kagan et al., 1958; Kagan & Moss, 1959). On the whole, all these findings point to a stability of achievement-motivated behavior between early childhood and adulthood which is surprisingly distinctive in comparison with other personality traits such as aggression, dependency, and passivity. Already at 10 years of age the future achievement behavior of the adult can be predicted quite well!

Crandall and collaborators, also from the Fels Institute, tried to clarify the developmental process via cross-sectional studies. They report that kindergarten children, striving more strongly toward achievement, turn less often to an adult for help and support (cf. Beller, 1957), and that achievement behavior at home and in kindergarten shows a certain consistency in this age group already (Crandall *et al.*, 1960b). In 6- and 9-year-olds such test behaviors as "value on intellectual achievement," "expectation of success," and "minimal goals set" correlate with observations of intensity of intellectual achievement behavior in a summer camp. The extent to which the correlations go back to variance contributed by age differences of 3 to 4 years, however, remains unexplained. The fact that these variables were unrelated to achievement motivation (*n* Achievement), does not mean much since the use of the usual TAT method (and Murray plates at that) is unsuitable for this age group. In a theoretical paper, Crandall, Katkovsky, and Preston (1960a) have defined certain important achievement-related variables (see the ones mentioned above) and their parameters. In line with the theory of "social learning" (Rotter, 1954) they see the real motivational goal as obtaining approval and avoiding disapproval (1960b). Implicit in such a notion is the inference that achievement motivation is *exclusively* a product of social learning and that achievement behavior originates entirely in reinforcement by social sanctions.

Such sanctions are effective reinforcers without any question. [Compare, for instance, the differing tendencies to make social contact after success and failure (Levin & Baldwin, 1959); the increase in persistence after competition and praise (Wolf, 1938).] We shall see that social sanctions have a decisive effect on the development of achievement motivation. However, they do not constitute the only possible kind of reinforcement. As stated above, the *sine qua non* for the origin of the motive is cognitive maturation, which causes the outcome of performance to be referred back to the self and, thus, to be experienced as an effect of one's own competence. Can there be any further doubt that the experience of competence has *in itself* a reinforcing value even for a small child, and that a feeling of efficacy (White, 1959) is sufficiently "rewarding"? If social approval or disapproval are aspired to, or avoided, exclusively for their own sake, one should no longer speak of achievement motivation. Usually, however, the approval of a relevant person involved is not an end in itself but rather an important measure of success (in addition to, or instead of, task-related measures of excellence)—a measure of success which is in the service of achievement motivation.

This can be corroborated by findings from the longitudinal studies of Kagan and Moss (1962; Moss & Kagan, 1961). Achievement behavior which is pursued for its own sake, and the kind intended to yield social approval, correlate so closely with each other (around .80), in both children and adults, that the value of differentiating between them seems questionable (at least to the extent that observers and interviewers cannot distinguish clearly between them). In any event, social approval or esteem should not be made into *the* goal of achievement motivation as Gottschaldt has suggested (1933, pp. 97 ff.). He proffers the seemingly obvious hypothesis that the origin of achievement behavior, particularly of the setting of levels of aspiration, depend upon the differentiation of a social frame of reference out of status hierarchies. No doubt such hierarchies provide important achievement-related standards of excellence of a social nature, but it has not been demonstrated that they are a *sine qua non,* in a causal sense, of achievement conflicts and level of aspiration, although this was assumed by Gottschaldt (1933, p. 106; 1961, p. 282) and his collaborators (Müller, 1958; Helm, 1962; Mehl, 1962). The assumption is actually contradicted by the appearance of failure conflicts and the formation of level of aspiration at the age of 3 or 4, presumably before the child could have developed much of a conception of status hierarchies.

A further questionable deduction from this viewpoint is the inference that absence of level of aspiration formation in

feeble-minded children (Helm, 1962), or the absence of experiences of success and failure (Gottschaldt, 1961) is due to
low *social* maturity. If Hoppe (1932, p. 355, ff.) and Gottschaldt (1933, pp. 99 ff.) were unable to observe experiences of
success and failure in feeble-minded children, it can only be
because the children were *cognitively* overtaxed by the task
of building a tower (cf. critically in this connection, Helm,
1962). Heckhausen and Wasna (1965) found that imbeciles,
with an attained intelligence level of 3 years and 6 months,
displayed all the symptoms of success, failure, and conflict
that can be found in the normal child when working in competition on a task the comprehension of which requires no higher
level of intelligence. The cognitive mastery of the requirements of the task is therefore absolutely essential; only with
such understanding can the child actually confront a level of
difficulty which is neither too easy nor too hard. If the child
understands but is not confronted by moderate difficulty, even
if he is normal, he does not experience success or failure as
Hoppe himself found (1930).

III. INDIVIDUAL DIFFERENCES: PARENTAL INFLUENCES

The findings cited sketch the general stages in the development of achievement motivation. Special conditions of
development should be separated from the general course of
development because they influence the accentuation of
achievement motivation in an individual within the schema
typical of a given stage; however, strictly speaking, they have
nothing to do with the origin or the existence of achievement
motivation *per se*. It is a universal "fact of life" just as the
maturational steps in cognitive development are. Through the
influence of depth psychology and learning theory, one has
the inclination to trace stage-specific behaviors back to a
particular cause. This is what Keister (1938) did when she
found "undesirable" reactions to failure, such as premature

giving up and outbursts of emotion, in some of her test group of 3- to 6-year-old children; she tried to overcome their reactions by "therapy" in the form of a long-term training program. But such reactions are characteristic of the developmental period of the younger children in this age group and decline regularly in older children (Heckhausen & Roelofsen, 1962). On the other hand, the "stage-specific" view of classical developmental psychology is in danger of overlooking individual differences and their causes (cf. Bandura, 1962, p. 242) which we will now pursue.

As a rule, extreme groups of Ss with high and low motivation, as determined by the TAT measure or other criteria (under- and overachievement in school), have been compared with respect to differences in parental child-rearing practices. Although the findings are intricate and at times appear to be contradictory because of the disparity in theoretical formulations and methods, some convergences are obvious (cf. McClelland, 1961, Chapter 9). Winterbottom (1058; also in McClelland et al., 1953), in her pioneering work, asked mothers of 8- to 10-year-old boys with low and high n Achievement scores at what age they expected their sons to be independent, competent in various areas, and observant of certain rules. Mothers of highly motivated boys, in comparison with mothers of less motivated boys, insisted more on independence during the first 8 years of age: they rewarded self-reliant mastery with more recognition and tender affection, and also insisted on earlier observance of rules which, however, were not as numerous as they were for the boys with low motivation.

Heckhausen and Kemmler (1957) used teachers' ratings of performance (both socially and at work) during the first weeks of school as a measure of motivation. Mothers of beginners who were mentally and socially ready for school, expected and desired independence and freedom of choice earlier in their sons than did mothers whose sons were not yet mentally and socially ready for school. What is involved here is a *child-centered* self-reliance: the mother leaves her child free to try to master an activity on his own and thereby faces a certain risk herself. As in Winterbottom's case, there was no difference between the two groups with respect to independence in routine skills which relieved the mother of caretaking jobs. In contrast to the findings on school readiness, Chance (1961) found that first-graders whose mothers pushed to early self-reliance actually progressed less quickly in reading and writing than one would have expected on the basis of their intellectual ability.

Feld (1960) reexamined Winterbottom's *S*s 6 years later. The achievement motivation of the then 14–16-year-old boys correlated, strangely enough, negatively with the value the mothers placed on independence in their sons at *this* age level! Evidently the attitude of the mothers reversed itself for the older school age level. Furthermore, it is notable that the failure anxiety (TAQ) of the sons at the time was related to the absence of early self-reliance training and to a correspondingly lower level of achievement motivation during the first years of school.

In a comparative study of different social class and ethnic groups, Rosen (1959) found that Winterbottom's findings are characteristic only of a middle-class sample. Independence in routine skills which relieve the parents of caretaking is demanded earlier than child-centered self-reliance in the lower social class. Such authoritarian, restrictive socialization practices result in low achievement motivation, no matter how early a more child-centered type of self-reliance is expected (cf. McClelland, 1961, pp. 345 ff.: comparison of Japanese, German, and Brazilian samples). This is confirmed in a cross-cultural study of 52 preliterate cultures by Child *et al.* (1958), who found that the achievement-related content of orally transmitted folklore is associated with dominant child rearing practices (as in an earlier study by McClelland &

Friedman, 1952). The more restrictive and more intent on obedience the child-rearing, the lower the amount of achievement content contained in the folk tales. Furthermore, it was shown that, contrary to McClelland and Friedman (1952), high achievement orientation is created less by early independence training than by the more direct transmittal of achievement-related value attitudes by the parents, whether they occurred in the form of reward or punishment for achievement in cultures "low in general indulgence" or in the form of a positive role model for achievement in cultures "high in general indulgence."

Relationships of this kind have also been established by Crandall and his collaborators (1960b) in their cross-sectional studies at the Fels Institute. Thus, the achievement behavior of 3- to 5-year-old kindergarten children correlates with the degree of positive reinforcement which they receive from their mothers (middle-class population) for their achievement efforts and strivings for recognition. Another study (Crandall, Dewey, Katkovsky, & Preston, 1964) produced more correlations between parental attitudes or reactions and outcome in an academic achievement test for daughters than for sons; the relationships are, however, trivial (e.g., between dissatisfaction with the child's competence and poor performance on an academic achievement test). Other investigations (Katkovsky, Preston, & Crandall, 1964a,b) have shown that parents apply the same expectations and evaluative attitudes toward achievement in their children as they do toward their own achievement. Furthermore, they interfere in various ways in order to transfer their own evaluative attitudes to their children; it is notable that the effect of this interference is more frequently visible in the child of the opposite sex.

Using the same population, Moss and Kagan (1961) obtained estimates of "maternal acceleration" directed at the child's development and ability to achieve during the first 10 years. Such acceleration attempts, even during the first 3 years of age, show important relationships with the prominence of achievement behavior in later adulthood; the same is true for comparable measures at ages 6 and 10. Based on maternal acceleration between the ages 6 and 10 it was possible to predict the achievement motivation scores (n Achievement) of sons 14½ years old and of daughters 25 years old.

Argyle and Robinson (1962) obtained similar findings in a comprehensive correlational study using English high school students. The level of parental demands for achievement, estimated by the students themselves, correlated with the strength of their own achievement motivation (n Achievement). This was true for mothers and sons, and particularly if there was stronger "identification" with the parents (i.e. greater similarity on the basis of semantic differentials).

Hayashi *et al.* (1962) have demonstrated that in Japan parents of highly motivated children attach more value to good education and to more education. Japanese mothers appear to expect more achievement-related self-reliance from their children than fathers do (and both parents expect more from their sons than from their daughters). They did not find a correlation between parental insistence on self-reliance and their children's achievement motivation. Hayashi and Yamaushi (1964) report just the reverse of Winterbottom's findings (1958). Mothers of low-motivated preschool children (3–6 years) make more demands than do mothers of highly motivated children by the age of 6. This relation reverses itself after the age of 7. That is, after the age of 7 mothers of the lows begin to make less demands than is found for the mothers of the highs. It still remains to be seen the extent to which this is true to the provisional nature of the indexes of self-reliance training or to some cultural peculiarities of this variable in Japan. The age levels of independence demands reported by Japanese mothers are considerably lower than age levels found in the United States (Winterbottom, 1958) and in Germany (Heckhausen & Kemmler, 1957). It looks as if Japanese mothers might be too premature in their independence demands and, thus, they miss the "critical period" for optimal training in independence. The notion of a critical period in independence training has recently been proposed by Veroff (1965).

Rosen (1962) has found Brazilian children to be much lower in achievement motivation than North American children, particularly if they are from the upper social strata. Brazilian parents are gentler and spoil their children more; they require self-reliance and readiness for achievement later and less rigorously than American parents. As part of an authoritarian, patriarchal family structure, they expect big things of their children without simultaneously making demands on them. This appears to develop inflated self-esteem, self-deceptiveness, and finally avoidance tendencies rather than a motivated readiness to achieve.

According to the above findings, one should distinguish between two directions in which the mother's child rearing may turn. She may either insist on early self-reliance in all matters or more specifically just on early readiness to achieve. In the latter instance, the results of several investigations have shown (Child et al., 1958; Crandall et al., 1960a, Argyle & Robinson, 1962; Krebs, 1958) that high Achievement motivation is not so meaningfully related to early self-reliance training as it is to lesser concern for conformity. However, it is noteworthy that early self-reliance training and achievement motivation both relate to conformity in the same way; the later the self-reliance training and the lower the achievement motivation, the more marked the tendency to conform. Furthermore, the intention behind the push to early development is important. A massive, premature pressure for achievement on the part of the parents indicates rather a cold rejection of the child's needs which is not intended to further the child's self-reliance for its own sake. It appears not to further but rather to prejudice achievement motivation, as Rosen found (1959).

This conclusion is supported by a finding of Hurley (1962).

College students, who are of the opinion that children should be exposed early to massive achievement pressure, have poor academic standing although they are no less intelligent than their less extreme and more successful peers. Even more convincing is Morrow and Wilson's (1961) study which involved a carefully selected sample. They used over- and underachievement in high school as a motivational measure. The parents of bright, high achievers in school engage more in sharing of activities, and are more approving, trusting, and affectionate with their children; they encourage achievement but do not exert pressure. For underachievers the picture is correspondingly the reverse (cf. Shaw & Dutton, 1962; however, cf. Crandall and co-workers', 1964, finding that stricter and colder mothers had more competent daughters). Robinowitz (1956) found that overachievement is connected with the student's confusion and doubt as to whether he is respected and accepted by his family and his peers. It is probable that here the increased achievement drive is in the service of a desire for more acceptance by the relevant ingroups (cf. Martire, 1956, and Steiner, 1957). Aside from Gordon (1959), McClelland (1961) and Nuttall (1964), no one seems to have taken the parents' achievement motivation into account. According to Gordon, mothers with low motivation provide moderate independence training, while among the highly motivated mothers one group strives for early independence and another group surprisingly prefers a later date. According to Nuttall, highly motivated Negro parents prefer to follow a nonauthoritarian type of child training. McClelland (1961) found that mothers with moderate levels of n Achievement tended to have sons with highest n Achievement.

Fortunately, one study exists which in a single research design deals with almost all the questions raised in the investigations just cited: with independence or achievement competence as the center of gravity in upbringing; with the nature and intensity of parental sanctions; and, finally, with the different roles of father and mother. The results of this investigation integrate the above-mentioned findings and may, therefore, serve to summarize them. Rosen and D' Andrade (1959) wanted to observe parental influence directly and, therefore, arranged for 9–11 year old boys to work at achievement tasks (such as building a tower with irregularly shaped blocks) at home in the presence of their parents. The boys were blindfolded and allowed to use only one hand in order to make it more likely that they would get help from their parents. On the basis of a preliminary TAT, the boys were divided into groups high and low on n Achievement that were carefully matched for other factors, such as intelligence and socioeconomic status. Both the parents of the highly motivated sons, as compared to the parents of the sons with low motivation, set higher levels of aspiration with respect to their son's abilities to achieve. The parents, particularly the mothers, showed more appreciation and warmth. The mothers of the sons with high motivation, in contrast to the fathers, rebuked them for failure, broke in with hints, instructions, and efforts to urge their sons on. The fathers looked on in a more detached and benevolent way. According to these findings, strong achievement motivation in boys is promoted in families characterized by high achievement-oriented levels of aspiration and by warmth and harmonious personal relations; and in families in which the mother stimulates achievement competence directly by positive and negative sanctions, while the father on the contrary respects and furthers the son's autonomy which he stimulates by a sympathetic attitude toward self-reliance.

These appear to be the conditions under which *high* achievement-related value attitudes of the parent generation are best transferred to, and preserved by, the following generation. The mother assumes the direct teaching role making use of the classic principles of learning, reinforcing desirable behavior with rewards, and eliminating undesirable behavior with punishment. It is she who calls forth an "affective change" (McClelland *et al.*, 1953, p. 69), a "steep expectation gradient" (Heckhausen, 1963a) following the successful or unsuccessful outcome of an achievement situation. Her importance, particularly in early childhood, must be rated very high (McClelland, 1958b).

The optimal role for the father is more that of a benevolent and attractive model. He leaves room for his son to develop independently while imitating him. If the father interferes in an authoritarian way, he seems to make the son dependent and to make it impossible for strong value attitudes to transfer to him (Strodtbeck, 1958; Bradburn, 1963). Possibilities for "identification" with, or imitation of, a model are of great importance here as they are for the formation of other personality characteristics. The understanding of the role of such processes in the formation of a motive presupposes a revision in the classic theory of learning, as Bandura (1962) has pointed out. Bandura and Mischel (1965), for instance, have shown that children modify their individual delay of reward pattern after they have observed an adult model who exhibited delay behavior that was counter to the children's pattern of delay behavior.[14]

IV. EFFECTS OF FAMILY STRUCTURE

The family as a small-group structure may also contain influences which further or hinder the development of strong achievement motivation. Birth order of siblings, size of the family, and intactness of the home have been shown to be important. American first-born children are more highly motivated (Atkinson & Miller, 1956), especially girls (Sampson, 1962). The reason may be that Western culture gives them more responsibility for younger siblings, or gives them more responsibility at an earlier period. In other cultures, such as India, and Japan, it is rather the younger, and the

---

[14] See note added in proof, page 162.

youngest, children who are more highly motivated (Mc-Clelland, 1961, p. 374). The influence of family size on the achievement motivation of boys varies with social class (Rosen, 1961). In the upper classes, medium-size families produce boys with the highest scores, whereas in the middle class, the smaller the family the larger the score. Large size of family appears to have an unfavorable effect in Classes I, II, and V.

Broken homes, or weak ties between the parents, hinder the development of high achievement motivation. Veroff *et al.* (1960) found this to be true for men in their representative sample of the United States population. In a longitudinal investigation, Thomae (1956) found similar unfavorable effects on academic and vocational achievement among German children born after World War II. Relatively fatherless societies (various forms of polygyny) or subcultures (so-called "serial monogamy" of the lower social strata) also produce children with low motivation (McClelland, 1961, p. 373; Mischel, 1961; Nuttall, 1964). Separation from the father before adolescence, however, favors high achievement motivation in such an authoritarian, patriarchal society as Turkey (Bradburn, 1963). Strodtbeck (1958) has shown for American society that too much achievement-related pressure by the father, which is found especially in the upper social stratum, results in an unintended effect: the son becomes dependent and develops low achievement motivation.

V. EFFECTS OF THE SOCIOCULTURAL MILIEU

We come finally to such group characteristics as social class, educational level, and religion which determine the achievement-related "climate" of everyday life as it unfolds in its over-all context. Since we have already discussed sociocultural frames of reference (cf. pp. 28 f.), we will only mention here once again that the upwardly mobile middle class favors the development of strong future-oriented achievement motivation (Douvan, 1956; Douvan & Adelson, 1958; Rosen, 1959, 1962; Veroff et al., 1960, 1966; Crockett, 1962; Cameron & Storm, 1965). Achievement-motivated behavior in children is positively correlated with the level of parents' education, especially the fathers' (Kagan & Moss, 1962). The relationship is particularly marked when the children become adults. Thus, for instance, the parental level of education is a better predictor of the child's future intelligence than is the mother's IQ. The relationship is easy to understand because the parents' level of education is expressed in the achievement-related content of everyday life in its sociocultural context, and from this the child picks up, takes over, and develops his value attitudes.

The influence of the religious milieu, as suggested by Max Weber (1904/1905), has repeatedly been found to be important (e.g., McClelland, Rindlisbacher, & DeCharms, 1955; Rosen, 1959; Carney & McKeachie, 1963). The Catholic developmental milieu appears to be less fertile for developing high achievement motivation. Although Catholic parents in Germany as well as in the United States do not demand independence from their children any later than do Protestant parents (Wendt, 1965, cited in McClelland, 1961, p. 360; Feld, cited in Veroff et al., 1962), they are more restrictive in their child-rearing practices (Wendt, 1965; cf. McClelland, 1961, p. 361); they place more value on obedience, orderliness, and cleanliness (Veroff et al., 1962); they punish more vigorously and provide more material rewards (D. R. Miller & Swanson, 1958, pp. 158–177). All this does not seem to favor the development of highly generalized self-reliant value attitudes. The more individualistic and more activistic the religious ethos of an environment, the more strongly achievement motivation is fostered, as McClelland has demonstrated (1961) with many separate findings.

Thus, it cannot be doubted that the outstanding achievements in business, the arts, and science in the United States and in Germany have been produced by more Protestants and fewer Catholics in relation to their numbers in the total population (cf. Knapp & Goodrich, 1952) or the greater proportion of Protestants among university graduates still existing in Germany (cf. *Amtsblatt der EKD,* 1954). Nevertheless, one finds that today the Protestant population in America and in Germany does not have higher achievement motivation than the Catholic population as long as one uses representative samples (Veroff *et al.*, 1960; McClelland, 1961) instead of biased samples, such as one obtains in studying not fully accultured American immigrants from Catholic countries (Rosen, 1959). According to the latest representative sample (Veroff, Feld, & Gurin, 1962), Catholics rank after Jews and, surprisingly, still ahead of Protestants (see above, p. 31). However, social class membership generally has a more decisive influence.

VI. CHANGES IN ADULTHOOD

As to changes in achievement motivation beyond early adulthood to date we know only that it is significantly lower in the fifth decade in a representative sample of the American population (Veroff *et al.*, 1960). The future time perspective of retired employees is shorter than for young employees (Böttcher, 1963). Krugman (1959) has described peculiarities in level of aspiration behavior beyond the seventieth year. The growing research on "human course of life" (C. Bühler, 1959) and, especially, on old age will be faced with a large number of questions [e.g., to mention just one, the achievement-related crisis of the aging person, the so-called "psychic bankruptcy caused by pensioning off" ("Pensionierungs-bankrott"; cf. Stauder, 1955)].

Kolb (1965) was able to improve school grades of under-achieving high-school boys (IQs above 120 and school grades below C) by giving them a training program designed to teach characteristics of the person with high achievement motivation. The improvement became manifest with students of high social class in a follow-up 1.5 years after the training, but failed to appear with students of low social class. A control group took part—as did the experimental group, too—in an academic summer-school program only. No grade improvement was noted in this group. McClelland (1964c, 1965a) is presently attempting, in research on Indian businessmen, to raise achievement motivation in adults through courses and subsequent follow-up contacts. If it is possible to influence the normative achievement motivation levels in this way, it would be of great practical importance for the economic growth of developing countries.

NOTE ADDED IN PROOF

For a detailed discussion of different factors that are operative in the development of motives the reader is referred to a theoretical paper by the author (Heckhausen, 1966). Five sources of motive development are formulated in an attempt to summarize research findings more fully, and need for achievement is taken as the motive paradigm. *Maturation of certain cognitive and motor functions* sets the stage for the first manifestations and, presumably, initiates a critical period of heightened susceptibility to influences. Already existing motives and role prescriptions may play the role of *precursor-motives* (e.g., independence motivation in the case of achievement motivation). The *amount of experienced discrepancies* that are motive-relevant in a given environment, *reinforcement learning,* and *identification learning* are considered further factors of great impact on motive development.

CHAPTER XIII

CONCLUDING REMARKS

The quantitative scoring of achievement motivation by means of the TAT method has not degenerated into a typology. On the contrary, it has tied together a ramified network of findings. Perhaps today we already know more about achievement motivation than about any other human motive although Ach and Lewin set the investigation in motion only about four decades ago.

This presentation has not followed the usual demarcation lines of textbook chapters in psychology. Comparable effects in various research areas suggest an over-all interconnectedness at the theoretical level. Experts may rightly find little profit in it as far as their subfield of interest is concerned, but they cannot deny its capacity to integrate findings in preparation for a basic theory of motivation. From their point of view, psychometricians must regret the test characteristics of the TAT method. It does not fulfill the requirements of a good test for individual diagnosis and probably never will. Its situational sensitivity has, fortunately, prevented it from being included in the category of diagnostic tests. This deficiency has proved to be an advantage for basic research. It has led to some unexpected findings and forced experimenters to follow them up. In consequence, it has become increasingly clear how intimately bound up motivation is with the interaction of enduring and situational factors.

The fruitfulness of the more recent methodological approaches is no longer in question. The anatomy of achievement motivation is presently being worked over in many places, not only in the United States but also in Japan, Australia, and Brazil, Germany, England, Italy, and the Netherlands. It seems likely that the yield in the future will continue to be worth the trouble taken. Furthermore, this area of research is always rewarding for those who like to cast doubt on the findings of others. For that purpose, one need only combine an unenlightened research design with slight deviations in method and gross failure to control experimental conditions. The "play" in interpretations is still too great, to be sure. Future research will have to continue to cut it down.

REFERENCES

Ach, N. *Über den Willensakt und das Temperament.* Leipzig: Quelle & Meyer, 1910.

Allport, G. W. *Personality.* New York: Holt, 1937.

Alper, Thelma G. Memory for completed and incompleted tasks as a function of personality: an analysis of group data. *J. abnorm. soc. Psychol.*, 1946, **41**, 403–420.

Alper, Thelma G. The interrupted task method in studies of selective recall: a reevaluation of some recent experiments. *Psychol. Rev.*, 1952, **59**, 71–88.

Alper, Thelma G. Predicting the direction of selective recall: its relation to ego strength and *n* Achievement. *J. abnorm. soc. Psychol.*, 1957, **55**, 149–165.

Alpert, R., & Haber, R. N. Anxiety in academic achievement situations. *J. abnorm. soc. Psychol.*, 1960, **61**, 207–215.

Amtsblatt der Evangelischen Kirche in Deutschland: 1954, **8**, Statistische Beilage No. 13. Religionszugehörigkeit und Berufsziele der Studierenden an den wissenschaftlichen Hochschulen in Westdeutschland und in West-Berlin im Wintersemester 1953/1954.

Anderson, R. C. Failure imagery in the fantasy of eighth graders as a function of three conditions of induced arousal. *J. educ. Psychol.*, 1962, **53**, 293–298.

Angelini, A. L. Studies in projective measurement of achievement motivation of Brazilian students, males and females. Proc. 15 intern. Congr., Brussels 1957. *Acta Psychol.*, 1959, **XV**, 359–360.

Argyle, M., & Robinson, P. Two origins of achievement motivation. *Brit. J. soc. clin. Psychol.*, 1962, **1**, 107–120.

Aronson, E. The need for achievement as measured by graphic expression. 1958 In J. W. Atkinson, 1958c. Pp. 249–265.

Atkinson, J. W. The achievement motive and recall of interrupted and completed tasks. *J. exp. Psychol.*, 1953, **46**, 381–390.

Atkinson, J. W. Motivational determinants of risk-taking behavior. *Psychol. Rev.*, 1957, **64**, 359–372. (Also in Atkinson, 1958c.)

Atkinson, J. W. Towards experimental analysis of human motivation in terms of motives, expectancies, and incentives. 1958. In J. W. Atkinson, 1958c. Pp. 288–305. (a)

Atkinson, J. W. Thematic apperceptive measurement of motives within the context of a theory of motivation. 1958. In J. W. Atkinson, 1958c. Pp. 596–616. (b)

Atkinson, J. W. (Ed.). *Motives in fantasy, action, and society.* Princeton, N.J.: Van Nostrand, 1958. (c)

Atkinson, J. W. Discussion of Dr. Lazarus' paper. In J. Kagan & G. S. Lesser (Eds.), *Contemporary issues in thematic apperceptive methods.* Springfield, Ill.: Charles C. Thomas, 1961. Pp. 72–82.

Atkinson, J. W. *An introduction to motivation.* Princeton, N.J.: Van Nostrand, 1964.

Atkinson, J. W., & Cartwright, D. Some neglected variables in contemporary conceptions of decision and performance. *Psychol. Rep.,* 1964, 14, 575–590.

Atkinson, J. W., & Litwin, G. H. Achievement motive and test anxiety conceived as motive to approach success and motive to avoid failure. *J. abnorm. soc. Psychol.,* 1960, 60, 52–63.

Atkinson, J. W., & Miller, D. R. Parental experiences in child training. Univer. of Michigan, 1956 (dittoed paper).

Atkinson, J. W. & Raphelson, A. C. Individual differences in motivation and behavior in particular situations. *J. Pers.,* 1956, 24, 349–363.

Atkinson, J. W., & Reitman, W. R. Performance as a function of motive strength and expectancy of goal attainment. *J. abnorm. soc. Psychol.,* 1956, 53, 361–366. (Also in Atkinson, 1958c).

Atkinson, J. W., Bastian, J. R., Earl, R. W., & Litwin, G. H. The achievement motive, goal-setting, and probability preferences. *J. abnorm. soc. Psychol.,* 1960, 60, 27–36.

Bandura, A. Social learning through imitation. In M. R. Jones (Ed.), *Nebraska symposium on motivation, 1962.* Lincoln, Neb.: Univer. of Nebraska Press, 1962. Pp. 211–269.

Bandura, A., & Mischel, W. Modification on self-imposed delay of reward through exposure to live and symbolic models. *J. Pers. soc. Psychol.,* 1965, 2, 698–705.

Barnette, W. L. A structured and semi-structured achievement measure applied to a college sample. *Educ. psychol. Measmt.,* 1961, 21, 647–656.

Barry, H., Bacon, M. K., & Child, I. L. A cross-cultural survey of some sex differences in socialization. *J. abnorm. soc. Psychol.,* 1957, 55, 327–332.

Bartenwerfer, H. Pulsrhythmikmerkmale als Indikatoren der psychischen Anspannung. *Psychol. Beitr.*, 1960, 4, 7–25.

Bartmann, T. Der Einfluss von Zeitdruck auf die Leistung und das Denkverhalten bei Volksschülern. *Psychol. Forsch.*, 1963, 27, 1–61.

Bartmann, T. *Denkerziehung im programmierten Unterricht.* München: Manz, 1965.

Beller, E. K. Dependency and autonomous achievement striving related to orality and anality in early childhood. *Child Develpm.*, 1957, 28, 287–315.

Bendig, A. W. Predictive and postdictive validity of need achievement measures. *J. educ. Res.*, 1958, 52, 119–120.

Bendig, A. W. Comparative validity of objective and projective measures of need achievement in predicting students' achievement in introductory psychology. *J. gen Psychol.*, 1959, 60, 237–243.

Berkowitz, L. The effects of observing violence. *Scientific Amer.*, 1964, 210, 35–41.

Berkowitz, L., & Rawlings, Edna. Effects of film violence on inhibitions against subsequent aggression. *J. abnorm. soc. Psychol.*, 1963, 66, 405–412.

Berlew, D. E. Interpersonal sensitivity and motive strength. *J. abnorm. soc. Psychol.*, 1961, 63, 390–394.

Berlew, D. E., & Williams, A. F. Interpersonal sensitivity under motive arousing conditions. *J. abnorm. soc. Psychol.*, 1964, 68, 150–159.

Berlyne, D. E. *Conflict, arousal, and curiosity.* New York: McGraw-Hill, 1960.

Bialer, I. Conceptualization of success and failure in mentally retarded and normal children. *J. Pers.*, 1961, 29, 303–320.

Birney, R. C. Thematic content and the cue characteristics of pictures. In J. W. Atkinson (Ed.), *Motives in fantasy, action, and society.* Princeton, N.J.: Van Nostrand, 1958. Pp. 630–643. (a)

Birney, R. C. The achievement motive and task performance: a replication. *J. abnorm. soc. Psychol.*, 1958, 56, 133–135. (b)

Birney, R. C. The reliability of the achievement motive. *J. abnorm. soc. Psychol.*, 1959, 58, 266–267.

Birney, R. C. Research on the achievement motive. In E. F. Borgatta & W. F. Lambert (Eds.), *Handbook of personality theory and research.* Chicago, Ill.: Rand McNally (in press).

Birney, R. C., Burdick, H., & Teevan, R. C. Analysis of TAT stories for hostile press thema. Paper read at EPA, April, 1961.

Böttcher, Helga. Über das Zeiterleben junger und alter Erzähler von TAT-Geschichten. Unpublished manuscript. Psychol. Inst. Univer. Münster, 1963.

Botha, Elize, & Close, Anne. Achievement motivation and speed of perception in relation to reading skill. *Percept. mot. Skills,* 1964, **19**, 74.

Bradburn, N. M. *n* Achievement and father dominance in Turkey. *J. abnorm. soc. Psychol.*, 1963, **67**, 464–468.

Brody, N. *n* Achievement, test anxiety and subjective probability of success in risk taking behavior. *J. abnorm. soc. Psychol.*, 1963, **66**, 413–418.

Broverman, D. M., Jordan, E. J., & Phillips, Leslie. Achievement motivation in fantasy and behavior. *J. abnorm. soc. Psychol.*, 1960, **60**, 374–378.

Brown, J. F. Über die dynamischen Eigenschaften der Realitäts- und Irrealitätsschichten. *Psychol. Forsch.*, 1933, **18**, 2–26.

Brown, J. S. Problems presented by the concept of acquired drives. In M. R. Jones (Ed.), *Nebraska symposium on motivation 1953*. Lincoln, Neb.: Univer. Nebraska Press, 1953. Pp. 1–21.

Brown, R. W. A determinant of the relationship between rigidity and authoritarianism. *J. abnorm. soc. Psychol.*, 1953, **48**, 469–476.

Bühler, Charlotte. *Der menschliche Lebenslauf als psychologisches Problem*. Göttingen: Hogrefe, 1959.

Bühler, K. *Abriss der geistigen Entwicklung des Kindes*. Leipzig: Quelle & Meyer, 1919.

Burdick, H. A. Need for achievement and schedules of variable reinforcement. *J. abnorm. soc. Psychol.*, 1964, **68**, 302–306.

Burnstein, E. Fear of failure, achievement motivation, and aspiring to prestigeful occupations. *J. abnorm. soc. Psychol.*, 1963, **67**, 189–193.

Burnstein, E., Moulton, R., & Liberty, P. Prestige *vs.* excellence as determinants of role attractiveness. *Amer. sociol. Rev.*, 1963, **28**, 212–219.

Butterfield, E. C. The interruption of tasks: methodological, factual, and theoretical issues. *Psychol. Bull.*, 1964, **62**, 309–322.

Cameron, Ann, & Storm, T. Achievement motivation in Canadian Indian middle- and working-class children. *Psychol. Rep.*, 1965, **16**, 459–463.

Carney, R. E. The effect of situational variables on the measurement of achievement motivation. (Prelim. draft). Indiana Univ., 1964. (a)

Carney, R. E. Validation of an objective measure of achievement motivation. (Preliminary draft). Indiana Univer., 1964. (b)

Carney, R. E. Research with a recently developed measure of achievement motivation. *Percept. mot. Skills*, 1965, **21**, 438.

Carney, R. E., & McKeachie, W. J. Religion, sex, social class, probability of success, and student personality. *J. sci. Stud. Religion*, 1963, **3**, 32–42.

Caron, A. J. Curiosity, achievement, and avoidant motivation as determinants of epistemic behavior. *J. abnorm. soc. Psychol.*, 1963, **67**, 535–549.

Caron, A. J., & Wallach, M. A. Recall of interrupted tasks under stress: A phenomenon of memory or learning? *J. abnorm. soc. Psychol.*, 1957, **55**, 372–381.

Caron, A. J., & Wallach, M. A. Personality determinants of repressive and obsessive reactions to failure-stress. *J. abnorm. soc. Psychol.*, 1959, **59**, 236–345.

Cartwright, D. The effect of interruption, completion, and failure upon the attractiveness of activities. *J. exp. Psychol.*, 1942, **31**, 1–16.

Chance, June E. Independence training and first graders' achievement. *J. consult. Psychol.*, 1961, **25**, 149–154.

Child, I. L., Storm, T., & Veroff, J. Achievement themes in folk tales related to socialization practice. 1958. In J. W. Atkinson, 1958c. Pp. 479–492.

Clark, R. A., & McClelland, D. C. A factor analytic integration of imaginative and performance measures of the need for achievement. *J. gen. Psychol.*, 1956, **55**, 73–83.

Clark, R. A., & Sensibar, Minda R. The relationship between symbolic and manifest projections of sexuality with some incidental correlates. *J. abnorm. soc. Psychol.*, 1955, **50**, 327–334. (Also in J. W. Atkinson, 1958c).

Clark, R. A., Teevan, R., & Ricciuti, H. N. Hope of success and fear of failure as aspects of need for achievement. *J. abnorm. soc. Psychol.*, 1956, **53**, 182–186. (Also in J. W. Atkinson, 1958c).

Cohen, J., & Hansel, M. Experimental risk-taking. *Jb. Psychol. Psychother.*, 1955, **3**, 382–388.

Cohen, J., & Hansel, C. E. M. *Glück und Risiko*. Frankfurt a.M.: Europ. Verlagsanstalt, 1961.

Cohen, A. R., & Zimbardo, P. G. An experiment on avoidance motivation. In J. W. Brehm & A. R. Cohen (Eds.), *Explorations in cognitive dissonance.* New York: Wiley, 1962. Pp. 143–151.

Cole, D., Jacobs, S., Zubok, Bea, Fagot, B., & Hunter, I. The relation of achievement imagery scores to academic performance. *J. abnorm. soc. Psychol.*, 1962, **65**, 208–211.

Cooper, L. M., & Howell, R. J. A reformulation of the "fear of failure" and "hope of success" concepts, as measured on McClelland's need achievement test. *J. soc. Psychol.*, 1961, **53**, 81–85.

Coopersmith, S.: A method for determining types of self-esteem. *J. abnorm. soc. Psychol.*, 1959, **59**, 87–94.

Coopersmith, S. Self-esteem and need achievement as determinants of selective recall and repetition. *J. abnorm. soc. Psychol.*, 1960, **60**, 310–317.

Crandall, V. J. & Rabson, Alice. Children's repetition choices in an intellectual achievement situation following success and failure. *J. genet. Psychol.*, 1960, **97**, 161–168.

Crandall, V. J., & Sinkeldam, C. Children's dependent and achievement behaviors in social situations and their perceptual field dependence. *J. Pers.*, 1964, **32**, 1–22.

Crandall, V. J., Solomon, D., & Kellaway, R. Expectancy statements and decision times as functions of objective probabilities and reinforcement values. *J. Pers.*, 1955, **24**, 192–203.

Crandall, V. J., Katkovsky, W., & Preston, Anne. A conceptual formulation for some research on children's achievement development. *Child Develpm.*, 1960, **31**, 787–797. (a)

Crandall, V. J., Preston, Anne, & Rabson, Alice. Maternal reactions and the development of independence and achievement behavior in young children. *Child Develpm.*, 1960, **31**, 243–251. (b)

Crandall, V. J., Dewey, Rachel, Katkovsky, W., & Preston, Anne. Parents' attitudes and behaviors and grade-school children's academic achievement. *J. genet. Psychol.*, 1964, **104**, 53–66.

Crockett, H. J. The achievement motive and differential occupational mobility in the United States. *Amer. sociol. Rev.*, 1962, **27**, 191–204.

Davids, A., & Sidman, J. A. A pilot study—impulsivity, time orientation, and delayed gratification in future scientists and in underachieving high school students. *Except. Children*, 1962, **29**, 170–174.

DeCharms, R., & Moeller, G. H. Values expressed in American children's readers: 1800–1950. *J. abnorm. soc. Psychol.*, 1962,

64, 136–142.

DeCharms, R., & Davé, Prafulachandra N. Hope of success, fear of failure, subjective probability, and risk-taking behavior. *J. Pers. soc. Psychol.*, 1965, 1, 558–568.

DeCharms, R., Morrison, W., Reitman, W., & McClelland, D. C. Behavioral correlates of directly and indirectly measured achievement motivation. In D. C. McClelland (Ed.), *Studies in motivation*. New York: Appleton, 1955. Pp. 414–423.

Dember, W. N., Nairne, F., & Miller, F. J. Further validation of the Alpert-Haber Achievement Anxiety Test. *J. abnorm. soc. Psychol.*, 1962, 65, 427–428.

Dembo, Tamara. Ärger als dynamisches Problem. *Psychol. Forsch.*, 1931, 15, 1–114.

Dennis, W. Are Hopi children noncompetitive? *J. abnorm. soc. Psychol.*, 1955, 50, 99–100.

Diggory, J. C., & Morlock, H. C. Level of aspiration, or probability of success? *J. abnorm. soc. Psychol.*, 1964, 69, 282–289.

Diller, L. Conscious and unconscious self-attitudes after success and failure. *J. Pers.*, 1954, 23, 1–12.

Douvan, Elizabeth. Social status and success strivings. *J. abnorm. soc. Psychol.*, 1956, 52, 219–223.

Douvan, Elizabeth, & Adelson, J. The psychodynamics of social mobility in adolescent boys. *J. abnorm. soc. Psychol.*, 1958, 56, 31–44.

Duffy, Elizabeth. The psychological significance of the concept of "arousal" or "activation." *Psychol. Rev.*, 1957, 64, 265–275.

Düker, H. *Psychologische Untersuchungen über freie und zwangsläufige Arbeit*. Leipzig: Barth, 1931.

Düker, H. Über ein Verfahren zur Untersuchung der psychischen Leistungsfähigkeit. *Psychol. Forsch.* 1949, 23, 10–24.

du Preez, P. D.: Judgment of time and aspects of personality, *J. abnorm. soc. Psychology*, 1964, 69, 228–233.

Easter, L. V., & Murstein, B. I. Achievement fantasy as a function of probability of success. *J. consult. Psychol.*, 1964, 28, 154–159.

Edwards, A. L. *Edwards Personal Preference Schedule*. New York: Psychol. Corp., 1954.

Edwards, W. The theory of decision-making. *Psychol. Bull.*, 1954, 51, 380–417.

Epstein, S. The measurement of drive and conflict in humans: theory and experiment. In M. R. Jones (Ed.), *Nebraska symposium on motivation 1962*. Lincoln, Neb.: Univer. Nebraska

Press, 1962. Pp. 127–209.

Eriksen, C. W. Psychological defenses and "ego strength" in the recall of completed and incompleted tasks. *J. abnorm. soc. Psychol.*, 1954, 49, 45–50.

Ertel, S. Die emotionale Natur des "semantischen Raumes." *Psychol. Forsch.*, 1964, 28, 1–32.

Escalona, Sybille. The effect of success and failure upon the level of aspiration and behavior in manic-depressive psychoses. *Univer. Iowa Stud. Child Welfare*, 1940, 16, 199–302.

Eysenck, H. J. *Dimensions of personality*. London: Routledge, 1947.

Eysenck, H. J. *The structure of human personality*. (2nd ed.). London: Methuen, 1960.

Eysenck, H. J. The measurement of motivation. *Scientific Amer.*, 1963, 208, 130–137.

Eysenck, H. J., & Maxwell, A. E. Reminiscence as a function of drive. *Brit. J. Psychol.*, 1961, 52, 43–52.

Eysenck, H. J., & Willett, R. A. Performance and reminiscence in a symbol substitution task as a function of drive. *Percept. mot. Skills*, 1962, 15, 389–390.

Fajans, Sara. Erfolg, Ausdauer und Aktivität beim Säugling und Kleinkind. *Psychol. Forsch.*, 1933, 17, 268–305.

Feather, N. T. Success probability and choice behavior. *J. exp. Psychol.*, 1959, 58, 257–266. (a)

Feather, N. T. Subjective probability and decision under uncertainty. *Psychol. Rev.*, 1959, 66, 150–164 (b)

Feather, N. T. The relationship of persistence at a task to expectation of success and achievement-related motives. *J. abnorm. soc. Psychol.*, 1961, 63, 552–561.

Feather, N. T. The study of persistence. *Psychol. Bull.*, 1962, 59, 94–115.

Feather, N. T. The relationship of expectation of success to reported probability, task structure, and achievement related motivation. *J. abnorm. soc. Psychol.*, 1963, 66, 231–238. (a)

Feather, N. T. Persistence at a difficult task with alternative task of intermediate difficulty. *J. abnorm. soc. Psychol.*, 1963, 66, 604–609. (b)

Feather, N. T. Mowrer's revised two-factor theory and the motive-expectancy-value model. *Psychol. Rev.*, 1963, 70, 500–515. (c)

Feather, N. T. The effect of differential failure on expectation of success, reported anxiety, and response uncertainty. *J. Pers.*, 1963, 31, 289–312. (d)

Feather, N. T. The relationship of expectation of success to need achievement and test anxiety. *J. Pers. soc. Psychol.*, 1965, 1, 118–126. (a)

Feather, N. T. Performance at a difficult task in relation to initial expectancies of success, test anxiety, and need achievement. *J. Pers.*, 1965, 33, 200–217. (b)

Feld, Sheila C. Studies in the origins of achievement strivings. *Dissertation Abstr. (Univer. Michigan)*, 1960, 20, 4707.

Ferdinand, W. Experimentelle Untersuchungen über den Einfluss der persönlichen Wichtigkeit des Materials auf das Behalten. *Psychol. Forsch.*, 1959, 25, 455–517.

Ferguson, Eva D. Ego involvement: a critical examination of some methodological issues. *J. abnorm. soc. Psychol.*, 1962, 64, 407–417.

Feshbach, S. The drive-reducing function of fantasy behavior. *J. abnorm. soc. Psychol.*, 1955, 50, 3–11.

Feshbach, S. The stimulating versus cathartic effects of a vicarious aggressive activity. *J. abnorm. soc. Psychol.*, 1961, 63, 381–385.

Festinger, L. A theoretical interpretation of shifts in level of aspiration. *Psychol. Rev.*, 1942, 49, 235–250.

Festinger, L. *Theory of cognitive dissonance.* Evanston, Ill · Row-Peterson, 1957.

Fisher, S. Achievement themes and directionality of autokinetic movement. *J. abnorm. soc. Psychol.*, 1961, 63, 64–68.

Frank, J. D. Some psychological determinants of the level of aspiration. *Amer. J. Psychol.*, 1935, 47, 285–293.

Frank, J. D. Level of aspiration test. In H. A. Murray (Ed.), *Explorations in personality.* New York: Oxford Univer. Press, 1938. Pp. 461–471.

Frank, L. K. Time perspectives. *J. soc. Phil.*, 1939, 4, 293–312.

French, Elizabeth G. Interrelation among some measures of rigidity under stress and nonstress conditions. *J. abnorm. soc. Psychol.*, 1955, 51, 114–118. (a)

French, Elizabeth G. Some characteristics of achievement motivation. *J. exp. Psychol.*, 1955, 50, 232–236. (Also in Atkinson, 1958c). (b)

French, Elizabeth G. Motivation as a variable in work-partner selection. *J. abnorm. soc. Psychol.*, 1956, 53, 96–99.

French, Elizabeth G. Development of a measure of complex motivation, 1958. In J. W. Atkinson, 1958c. Pp. 242–248. (a)

French, Elizabeth G. The interaction of achievement motivation and ability in problem-solving success. *J. abnorm. soc. Psychol.*, 1958, **57**, 306–309. (b)

French, Elizabeth G., & Lesser, G. S. Some characteristics of the achievement motivation in women. *J. abnorm soc. Psychol.*, 1964, **68**, 119–128.

French, Elizabeth G., & Thomas F. H. The relation of achievement motivation to problem-solving effectiveness. *J. abnorm. soc. Psychol.*, 1958, **56**, 45–48.

Freud, S. *Die Traumdeutung.* (1900). Ges.Werke, II/III. London: Imago, 1942.

Freud, S. *Der Dichter und das Phantasieren.* (1908). Ges. Werke, VII. London: Imago, 1941.

Fuchs, R. *Gewissheit, Motivation und bedingter Reflex.* Meisenheim/Glan: Hain, 1954.

Fuchs, R. Funktionsanalyse der Motivation. (Tübinger Symposion über Motivation). *Z. exp. angew. Psychol.*, 1963, X, 626–645.

Gardner, J. W. The relation of certain personality variables to level of aspiration. *J. Psychol.*, 1940, **9**, 191–206.

Glixman, A. F. An analysis of the use of the interruption-technique in experimental studies of "repression." *Psychol. Bull.*, 1948, **45**, 491–506.

Götzl, H. Beziehungen zwischen Leistungsmotivation, Zeitperspektive und Zeigarnik-Effekt. Unpublished manuscript, Psychol. Inst. Univer. Münster, 1960.

Goldin, P. C. Experimental investigation of selective memory and the concept of repression and defense: a theoretical synthesis. *J. abnorm. soc. Psychol.*, 1964, **69**, 365–380.

Gordon, J. E. Relationships among mothers' *n* achievement, independence training attitudes, and handicapped children's performance. *J. consult. Psychol.*, 1959, **23**, 207–212.

Gottschaldt, K. *Der Aufbau des kindlichen Handelns.* Leipzig: Barth, 1933.

Gottschaldt, K. Diskussionsbeitrag zur Entwicklung des Leistungsverhaltens. *Z. Psychol.*, 1961, **165**, 281–283.

Gough, H. G. *California Psychological Inventory.* Palo Alto, Calif.: Consulting Psychologists Press, 1957.

Gough, H. G. Achievement in the first course in psychology as predicted from the California Psychological Inventory. *J. Psychol.*, 1964, **57**, 419–430.

Gould, R., & Kaplan, N. The relationship of "level of aspiration" to academic and personality factors. *J. soc. Psychol.*, 1940, 11, 31–40.

Green, D. R. Volunteering and the recall of interrupted tasks. *J. abnorm. soc. Psychol.*, 1963, 66, 397–401.

Green, Helen B., & Knapp, R. H. Time adjustment, aesthetic preference, and need for achievement. *J. abnorm. soc. Psychol.*, 1959, 58, 140–142.

Greenbaum, C. W., Cohn, A., & Krauss, R. M. Choice, negative information, and attractiveness of tasks. *J. Pers.*, 1965, 33, 46–59.

Greenberg, Pearl J. Competition in children: an experimental study. *Amer. J. Psychol.*, 1932, 44, 221–248.

Groesbeck, B. L. Toward description of personality in terms of configuration of motives. In J. W. Atkinson, 1958c. Pp. 383–399.

Grünewald, G., & Mücher, H. Über den Einfluss zentraler Funktionsaktivierung auf die Schreibmotorik. *Z. Psychopharmakol.*, 1964, 5, 372–389.

Guérin, Françoise. Aperçu général sur les tests et les expériences de niveau d' aspiration. *Rev. Psychol. appl.*, 1958, 8, 221–251.

Haber, R. N., & Alpert, R. The role of situation and picture cues in projective measurement of the achievement motive. 1958. In J. W. Atkinson, 1958c. Pp. 644–663.

Hancock, J. G., & Teevan, R. C. Fear of failure and risk-taking behavior. *J. Pers.*, 1964, 32, 200–209.

Hardy, K. R. Determinants of conformity and attitude change. *J. abnorm. soc. Psychol.*, 1957, 54, 289–294.

Hayashi, T., & Habu, K. A research on achievement motive: an experimental test of the "thought sampling" method by using Japanese students. *Japanese Psychol. Res.*, 1962, 4, 30–42. (a)

Hayashi, T., & Habu, K. Achievement motivation and its relation to anxiety tendencies. *Bull Kyoto Gakugei Univer.*, Ser. A, 1962, 21, 21–28. (b)

Hayashi, T., & Yamaushi, K. The relation of children's need for achievement to their parents' home discipline in regard to independence and mastery. *Bull. Kyoto Gakugei Univer.*, Ser. A, 1964, 25, 31–40.

Hayashi, T., Okamoto, N., & Habu, K. Children's achievement motivation and its relation to intelligence, school achievements, anxiety tendencies, and parents-child relations. *Bull. Kyoto Gakugei Univer.*, Ser. A, 1962, 21, 16–20.

Hebb, D. O. Drives and the C.N.S. (conceptual nervous system). *Psychol. Rev.*, 1955, 62, 243–254.

Heckhausen, H. Motivationsanalyse der Anspruchsniveau-Setzung. *Psychol. Forsch.*, 1955, **25**, 118–154.

Heckhausen, H. Leistungsmotivation, Konflikt und Zielsetzung. *Ber. 21. Kongr. Deutsch. Ges. Psychol., 1957.* Göttingen: Hogrefe, 1958, **21**, 193–195.

Heckhausen, H. Die Problematik des Projektionsbegriffs und die Grundlagen und Grundannahmen des Thematischen Auffassungstests. *Psychol. Beitr.*, 1960, **V**, 53–80.

Heckhausen, H. Eine Rahmentheorie der Motivation in zehn Thesen. *Z. exp. angew. Psychol.*, 1963, **X**, 604–626. (a)

Heckhausen, H. *Hoffnung und Furcht in der Leistungsmotivation.* Meisenheim/Glan: Hain, 1963. (b)

Heckhausen, H. Über die Zweckmässigkeit einiger Situationsbedingungen bei der inhaltsanalytischen Erfassung der Motivation. *Psychol. Forsch.*, 1964, **27**, 244–259. (a)

Heckhausen, H. Entwurf einer Psychologie des Spielens. *Psychol. Forsch.*, 1964, **27**, 225–243. (b)

Heckhausen, H. Einflüsse der Erziehung auf die Motivationsgenese. In T. Herrmann (Ed.), *Psychologie der Erziehungsstile.* Göttingen: Hogrefe, 1966. Pp. 131–169.

Heckhausen, H., & Kemmler, Lilly. Entstehungsbedingungen der kindlichen Selbständigkeit. *Z. exp. angew. Psychol.*, 1957, **IV**, 603–622.

Heckhausen, H., & Roelofsen, Irmgard. Anfänge und Entwicklung der Leistungsmotivation: (I) im Wetteifer des Kleinkindes. *Psychol. Forsch.*, 1962, **26**, 313–397.

Heckhausen, H., & Seibt, Gabriele. Anfänge und Entwicklung der Leistungsmotivation: (III) im freien Spiel des Kleinkindes. (in preparation).

Heckhausen, H., & Wagner, Inge. Anfänge und Entwicklung der Leistungsmotivation: (II) in der Zielsetzung des Kleinkindes. Zur Genese des Anspruchsniveaus. *Psychol. Forsch.*, 1965, **28**, 179–245.

Heckhausen, H., & Wasna, Maria. Erfolg und Misserfolg in Leistungswetteifer des imbezillen Kindes. *Psychol. Forsch.*, 1965, **28**, 391–421.

Heckhausen, H., Ertel, S., & Kiekheben-Roelofsen, Irmgard. Die Anfänge der Leistungsmotivation im Wetteifer des Kleinkindes. *Tonfilm. Inst. Wiss. Film*, Göttingen, 1964.

Heider, F. *The Psychology of interpersonal relations.* New York: Wiley, 1958.

Helm, J. Über den Einfluss affektiver Spannungen auf das Denk-
   handeln. Z. *Psychol.*, 1954, **157**, 23–105.
Helm, J. Über die Wirkung von Erfolgsserien auf das Denkhandeln
   und die Leistung. Z. *Psychol.*, 1958, **162**, 3–114.
Helm, J. Beitrag zum Problem des Zielsetzungsverhaltens bei
   Debilen. Z. *Psychol.*, 1962, **166**, 167–181.
Henle, Mary. On activity in the goal region. *Psychol. Rev.*, 1956,
   63, 299–302.
Hillgruber, A. Fortlaufende Arbeit und Willensbetätigung. *Unters.
   Psychol. Phil.*, 1912, **1**, Heft 6.
Himelstein, P., & Kimbrough, W. W. Reliability of French's "Test of
   Insight." *Educ. psychol. Measmt.*, 1960, **20**, 737–741.
Himelstein, P., Eschenbach, A. E., & Carp, A. Interrelationships
   among three measures of need achievement. *J. consult. Psychol.*,
   1958, **22**, 451–452.
Hoffman, M. L., Mitsos, S. B., & Protz, R. E. Achievement striving,
   social class, and test anxiety. *J. abnorm. soc. Psychol.*, 1958, **56**,
   401–403.
Honigfeld, G., & Spigel, I. M. Achievement motivation and field
   independence. *J. consult. Psychol.*, 1960, 24, 550–551.
Hoppe, F. Erfolg und Misserfolg. *Psychol. Forsch.*, 1930, 14, 1–62.
Hoppe, F. Versuche über Erfolgs- und Misserfolgserlebnisse psycho-
   pathischer und schwachsinniger Kinder. *Ber. 12. Kongr. Deutsch.
   Ges. Psychol.* Jena: Fischer, 1932, **12**, 353–356.
Howard, T. C. The relation between psychological and mathematical
   probability. *Amer. J. Psychol.*, 1963, **76**, 335.
Hoyos, C. Graf. Motivationspsychologische Aspekte des Risikover-
   haltens. *Ber. 23. Kongr. Deutsch. Ges. Psychol.*, 1962. Göttingen:
   Hogrefe, 1963, **23**, 151–152.
Hoyos, C. Graf. Motivationspsychologische Untersuchungen von
   Kraftfahrern mit dem TAT nach McClelland. *Arch. ges. Psychol.*,
   1965, Supplementary Vol. 7.
Hurley, J. R. The Iowa Picture Interpretation Test: a multiple choice
   variation of the TAT. *J. consult. Psychol.*, 1955, **19**, 372–376.
Hurley, J. R. Achievement imagery and motivational instructions as
   determinants of verbal learning. *J. Pers.*, 1957, **25**, 274–282.
Hurley, J. R. Achievement pressure: an attitudinal correlate of
   college course grades. *Psychol. Rep.*, 1962, **10**, 695–702.
Irwin, F. W. The realism of expectations. *Psychol. Rev.*, 1944, **51**,
   120–126.
Isaacson, R. L. Relation between *n* achievement, test anxiety, and

curricular choices. *J. abnorm. soc. Psychol.*, 1964, **68**, 447–452.

Jäger, A. O. Einige emotionale, conative und zeitliche Bedingungen des Erinnerns. *Z. exp. angew. Psychol.*, 1959, **VI**, 737–765.

Jessor, R., & Readio, J. The influence of the value of an event upon the expectancy of its occurrence. *J. gen Psychol.*, 1957, **56**, 219–228.

Johnson, Miriam M. Sex role learning in the nuclear family. *Child Develpm.*, 1963, **34**, 319–333.

Johnston, R. A. The effects of achievement imagery on maze-learning performance. *J. Pers.*, 1955, **24**, 145–152.

Johnston, R. A. A methodological analysis of several revised forms of the Iowa Picture Interpretation Test. *J. Pers.*, 1957, **25**, 283–293.

Jucknat, Margarete. Leistung, Anspruchsniveau und Selbstbewusstsein. *Psychol. Forsch.*, 1937, **22**, 89–179.

Junker, Erika. Über unterschiedliches Behalten eigener Leistungen. *Psychol. Arbeiten, 6.* Frankfurt a.M.: Kramer, 1960.

Kagan, J., & Moss, H. A. Stability and validity of achievement fantasy. *J. abnorm. soc. Psychol.*, 1959, **58**, 357–364.

Kagan, J., & Moss, H. A. *Birth to maturity.* New York: Wiley, 1962.

Kagan, J., Sontag, L. W., Baker, C. T., & Nelson, Virginia L. Personality and IQ change. *J. abnorm. soc. Psychol.*, 1958, **56**, 261–266.

Kaltenbach, J. E., & McClelland, D. C. Achievement and social status in three small communities. In D. C. McClelland *et al.* (Eds.), *Talent and society.* Princeton, N.J.: Van Nostrand, 1958. Pp. 112–134.

Kardiner, A. *Psychological frontiers of society.* New York: Columbia Univer. Press, 1945.

Karolchuck, Patricia, & Worell, L. Achievement motivation and learning. *J. abnorm. soc. Psychol.*, 1956, **53**, 255–257.

Kassarjian, H. H. Success, failure, and personality. *Psychol. Rep.*, 1963, **13**, 567–574.

Katchmar, L. T., Ross, S., & Andrews, T. G. Effects of stress and anxiety on performance of a complex verbal-coding task. *J. exp. Psychol.*, 1958, **55**, 559–563.

Katkovsky, W., Preston, Anne, & Crandall, V. J. Parents' achievement attitudes and their behavior with their children in achievement situations. *J. genet. Psychol.*, 1964, **104**, 105–121. (a)

Katkovsky, W., Preston, Anne, & Crandall, V. J. Parents' attitudes toward their personal achievements and toward the achievement behaviors of their children. *J. genet. Psychol.*, 1964, **104**, 67–82. (b)

Katona, G. *Organizing and memorizing*. New York: Columbia Univer. Press, 1940.

Katz, D. Psychologie des Sicherheitsmarginals. *Acta Psychol.*, 1953, 9, 255–273.

Katz, F. M. The meaning of success: some differences in value systems of social classes. *J. soc. Psychol.*, 1964, **62**, 141–148.

Kausler, D. H., & Trapp, E. P. Achievement motivation and goal-setting behavior on a learning task. *J. exp. Psychol.*, 1958, **55**, 575–578.

Keister, Mary E. The behavior of young children in failure: an experimental attempt to discover and to modify undesirable responses of preschool children to failure. *Univer. Iowa Stud. Child Welfare*, 1938, **14**, 27–82.

Kimble, G. A. Evidence for the role of motivation in determining the amount of reminiscence in pursuit rotor learning. *J. exp. Psychol.*, 1950, **40**, 248–253.

Kissel, S., & Littig, L. W. Test anxiety and skin conductance. *J. abnorm. soc. Psychol.*, 1962, **65**, 276–278.

Klamma, Margaret. Über das Selbermachenwollen und Ablehnen von Hilfen bei Kleinkindern. Unpublished manuscript., Psychol. Inst. Münster, 1957.

Klauer, K. J. Überforderung bei Zeichenaufgaben. *Arch ges. Psychol.*, 1961, 113, 167–221.

Knapp, R. H. *n* Achievement and aesthetic preference. 1958. In J. W. Atkinson, 1958c. Pp. 367–372.

Knapp, R. H. Attitudes toward time and aesthetic choice. *J. soc. Psychol.*, 1962, **56**, 79–87.

Knapp, R. H., & Garbutt, J. T. Time imagery and the achievement motive. *J. Pers.*, 1958, **26**, 426–434.

Knapp, R. H., & Garbutt, J. T. Variation in the time description and need achievement. *J. soc. Psychol.*, 1965, **67**, 269–272.

Knapp, R. H., & Goodrich, H. B. *Origins of American scientists*. Chicago: Chicago Univer. Press, 1952.

Knapp, R. H., & Green, Helen B. The judgment of music-filled intervals and *n* Achievement. *J. soc. Psychol.*, 1961, **54**, 263–267.

Knapp, R. H., & Green, Helen B. Personality correlates of success imagery. *J. soc. Psychol.*, 1964, **62**, 93–99.

Kolb, D. A. Achievement motivation training for under-achieving high-school boys. *J. Pers. soc. Psychol.*, 1965, **2**, 783–792.

Kohn, M. L. Social class and the exercise of parental authority. *Amer. sociol. Rev.*, 1959, **24**, 352–366.

Kornadt, H.-J. Thematische Apperzeptionsverfahren. *Handbuch Psychol.*, Vol. 6. Göttingen: Hogrefe, 1963. Pp. 635–684.

Krebs, A. M. Two determinants of conformity: age of independence training and *n* Achievement. *J. abnorm. soc. Psychol.*, 1958, **56,** 130–131.

Krugman, A. D. A note on level-of-aspiration behavior and aging. *J. Geront.*, 1959, 14, 222–225.

Krumboltz, J. D. Measuring achievement motivation: A review. *J. counsel. Psychol.*, 1957, 4, 191–198.

Krumboltz, J. D., & Farquhar, W. W. Reliability and validity of the *n* Achievement test. *J. consult. Psychol.*, 1957, **21,** 226–228.

Künkel, F. *Einführung in die Charakterkunde.* Leipzig: Hirzel, 1928.

Lambert, W. E., & Klineberg, O. Cultural comparisons of boys' occupational aspirations. *Brit. J. soc. Psychol.*, 1963, **2,** 56–65.

Lazarus, R. S. A substitutive-defensive conception of apperceptive fantasy. In J. Kagan & G. S. Lesser (Eds.), *Contemporary issues in thematic apperceptive methods.* Springfield, Ill.: Charles C. Thomas, 1961. Pp. 51–71.

Lazarus, R. S., Deese, J., & Osler, Sonia F. The effects of psychological stress upon performance. *Psychol. Bull.*, 1952, **49,** 293–312.

Lazarus, R. S., Baker, R. W., Broverman, D. M., & Mayer, J. Personality and psychological stress. *J. Pers.*, 1957, **25,** 559–577.

Lersch, P. *Aufbau des Charakters.* Leipzig: Barth, 1938.

Leshan, L. L. Time variation and social class. *J. abnorm. soc. Psychol.*, 1952, **47,** 589–592.

Lesser, G. S. Conflict analysis of fantasy aggression. *J. Pers.*, 1958, **26,** 29–41.

Lesser, G. S., Krawitz, Rhoda N., & Packard, Rita. Experimental arousal of achievement motivation in adolescent girls. *J. abnorm. soc. Psychol.*, 1963, **66,** 59–66.

Leuba, C. An experimental study of rivalry in young children. *J. comp. Psychol.*, 1933, **16,** 367–378.

Levin, H., & Baldwin, A. L. Pride and shame in children. In M. R. Jones (Ed.), *Nebraska symposium on motivation 1959.* Lincoln, Neb.: Univer. of Nebraska Press. 1959. Pp. 138–173.

Lewin, K. Vorsatz, Wille und Bedürfnis. *Psychol. Forsch.*, 1926, **7,** 294–385.

Lewin, K. *A dynamic theory of personality.* New York: McGraw-Hill, 1935.

Lewin, K. Behavior and the development as a function of the total situation. In L. Carmichael (Ed.), *Manual of child psychology.* New York: Wiley, 1946. Pp. 791–844.

Lewin, K. Field theory in social psychology. In M. H. Marx (Ed.), *Psychological theory.* New York: Macmillan, 1951. Pp. 527–542.

Lewin, K. Zeitperspektive und Moral. In K. Lewin (Ed.), *Die Lösung sozialer Konflikte.* Bad Nauheim: Christian, 1953. Pp. 152–180.

Lewin, K., Dembo, Tamara, Festinger, L., & Sears, Pauline S. Level of aspiration. In J. McV. Hunt (Ed.), *Personality and behavior disorders, Vol. I.* New York: Ronald, 1944. Pp. 333–378.

Lewis, Helen B., & Franklin, Muriel, An experimental study of the role of the ego in work. II. The significance of task-orientation in work. *J. exp. Psychol.,* 1944, 34, 195–215.

Lindsley, D. B. Psychophysiology and motivation. In M. R. Jones (Ed.), *Nebraska symposium on motivation 1957.* Lincoln, Neb.: Univer. of Nebraska Press, 1957. Pp. 44–105.

Littig, L. W. The effect of motivation on probability preference and subjective personality. Unpublished doctoral dissertation. Univer. of Michigan, Ann Arbor, 1959.

Littig, L. W. Effect of anxiety on real and ideal vocational aspiration among grammar school boys. *Nature,* 1963, **199,** No. 4899, 1214–1215. (a)

Littig, L. W. Effects of motivation on probability preferences. *J. Pers.,* 1963, **31,** 417–427. (b)

Littig, L. W., & Yeracaris, C. A. Academic achievement correlates of achievement and affiliation motivations. *J. Psychol.,* 1963, **55,** 115–119.

Littig, L. W., & Yeracaris, C. A. Achievement motivation and intergenerational occupational mobility. *J. Pers. soc. Psychol.,* 1965, **1,** 386–389.

Litwin, G. H. Motives and expectancy as determinants of preference for degrees of risk. Unpublished doctoral dissertation Univer. of Michigan, 1958.

Litwin, G. H. A note on achievement motivation of salesmen and sales managers. Cambridge, Mass.: Harvard Business School, 1964.

Lowell, E. L. The effect of need for achievement on learning and speed of performance. *J. Psychol.,* 1952, 33, 31–40.

Luchins, A. R. Mechanization in problem solving. The effect of Einstellung. *Psychol. Monogr.,* 1942, 54, No. 6 (Whole No. 248).

McArthur, C. C. The effects of need for achievement on the content of TAT stories: a re-examination. *J. abnorm. soc. Psychol.*, 1953, 48, 532–536. (Also in Atkinson, 1958c).

McCall, R. J. Invested self-expression: a principle of human motivation. *Psychol. Rev.*, 1963, 70, 289–303.

McClelland, D. C. *Personality.* New York: Sloane, 1951.

McClelland, D. C. Measuring motivation in fantasy. In D. C. McClelland (Ed.), *Studies in motivation.* New York: Appleton, 1955. Pp. 401–413.

McClelland, D. C. Risk-taking in children with high and low need for achievement. 1958. In J. W. Atkinson, 1958c. Pp. 306–321. (a)

McClelland, D. C. The importance of early learning in the formation of motives. 1958. In J. W. Atkinson, 1958c. Pp. 437–452. (b)

McClelland, D. C. The use of measures of human motivation in the study of society. 1958. In J. W. Atkinson, 1958c. Pp. 518–552. (c)

McClelland, D. C. Methods of measuring human motivation. In J. W. Atkinson, 1958c. Pp. 7–42. (d)

McClelland, D. C. *The achieving society.* Princeton, N.J.: Van Nostrand, 1961.

McClelland, D. C. Achievement drive and economic growth. In D. C. McClelland (Ed.), *Roots of consciousness.* Princeton, N.J.: Van Nostrand, 1964. Pp. 16–45. (a)

McClelland, D. C. The United States and Germany: a comparative study of national character. In D. C. McClelland (Ed.), *Roots of consciousness.* Princeton, N.J.: Van Nostrand, 1964. Pp. 62–92. (b)

McClelland, D. C. Recent research at the Center for Research in Personality. Unpublished manuscript, Harvard Univ., 1964. (c)

McClelland, D. C. The psychodynamics of creative physical scientists. In D. C. McClelland (Ed.), *Roots of consciousness.* Princeton, N.J.: Van Nostrand, 1964. Pp. 146–181. (d)

McClelland, D. C. Toward a theory of motive acquisition. *Amer. Psychologist*, 1965. 321–333. (a)

McClelland, D. C. *n* Achievement and entrepreneurship: A longitudinal study. *J. Pers. soc. Psychol.*, 1965, 1, 389–392. (b)

McClelland, D. C., & Apicella, F. S. A functional classification of verbal reactions to experimentally induced failure. *J. abnorm. soc. Psychol.*, 1945, 40, 376–390.

McClelland, D. C., & Apicella, F. S. Reminiscence following experimentally induced failure. *J. exp. Psychol.*, 1947, 37, 159–169.

McClelland, D. C., & Friedman, G. A. A cross-cultural study of the relationship between child rearing practices and achievement appearing in folk tales. In G. E. Swanson, T. M. Newcomb & E. L. Hartley (Eds.), *Readings in social psychology*. New York: Holt, 1952.

McClelland, D. C., & Liberman, A. M. The effects of need for achievement on recognition of need-related words. *J. Pers.*, 1949, **18**, 236–251.

McClelland, D. C., Atkinson, J. W., Clark, R. A., & Lowell, E. L. *The achievement motive*. New York: Appleton, 1953.

McClelland, D. C., Rindlisbacher, A., & DeCharms, R. Religious and other sources of parental attitudes toward independence training. In D. C. McClelland (Ed.), *Studies in motivation*. New York: Appleton, 1955.

McClelland, D. C., Baldwin, A. L., Bronfenbrenner, U., & Strodtbeck, F. L. *Talent and society*. Princeton, N.J.: Van Nostrand, 1958. (a)

McClelland, D. C., Knapp, R. H., Sturr, J., & Wendt, H. W. Obligations to self and society in the United States and Germany. *J. abnorm. soc. Psychol.*, 1958, **56**, 245–255. (b)

McKeachie, W. J. Motivation, teaching methods, and college learning. In M. R. Jones (Ed.), *Nebraska symposium on motivation 1961*. Lincoln. Neb. Univer of Nebraska Press, 1961. Pp. 111–142.

McKeachie, W. J., Pollie, D., & Speisman, J. Relieving anxiety in classroom examinations. *J. abnorm. soc. Psychol.*, 1955, **50**, 93–98.

McKee, J., & Leader, Florence B. The relationship of socio-economic status and aggression to the competitive behavior of preschool children. *Child Develpm.*, 1955, **26**, 135–142.

Maddox, H. Advice on how-to-study versus the actual practices of university students. *Percept. mot. Skills.*, 1963, **16**, 202.

Mahler, Wera. Ersatzhandlungen verschiedenen Realitätsgrades. *Psychol. Forsch.*, 1933, **18**, 27–89.

Mahone, C. H. Fear of failure and unrealistic vocational aspiration. *J. abnorm. soc. Psychol.*, 1960, **60**, 253–261.

Malmo, R. B. Activation: a neurophysiological dimension. *Psychol. Rev.*, 1959, **66**, 367–386.

Mandler, G., & Sarason, S. B. A study of anxiety and learning. *J. abnorm. soc. Psychol.*, 1952, **47**, 166–173.

Marlowe, D. Relationships among direct and indirect measures of the achievement motive and overt behavior. *J. consult. Psychol.*, 1959, **23**, 329–332.

Marrow, A. J. Goal tensions and recall. Part 2. *J. gen. Psychol.*, 1938, 19, 37–64.

Martire, J. G. Relationships between the self concept and differences in the strength and generality of achievement motivation. *J. Pers.*, 1956, 24, 364–375.

Mehl, J. Über Erfolge und Misserfolge im Leistungs- und Zufallsbereich. *Z. Psychol.*, 1962, 167, 177–267.

Melikian, L. H. The relationship between Edward's and McClelland's measures of achievement motivation. *J. consult. Psychol.*, 1958, 22, 296–298.

Merz, F., Weber, A., & Wieja, K. Individuelle Risikobereitschaft. *Final report on research program No. 4014.* Luxemburg: Hohe Behörde der Montanunion. Unpublished manuscript, 1963.

Metzger, W. *Psychologie* (2nd ed.). Darmstadt: Steinkopff, 1954.

Metzger, W. *Schöpferische Freiheit* (2nd ed.). Frankfurt a.M.: Kramer, 1962.

Meyer, H. H., Walker, W. B., & Litwin, G. H. Motive patterns and risk preferences associated with entrepreneurship. *J. abnorm. soc. Psychol.*, 1961, 63, 570–574.

Meyer, W.-U. Heckhausen, H., & Kemmler, Lilly. Validierungskorrelate der inhaltsanalytisch erfassten Leistungsmotivation guter und schwacher Schüler des dritten Schuljahres. *Psychol. Forsch.*, 1965, 28, 301–328.

Mierke, K. Direktions- und Motivationskräfte im Leistungsvollzug. *Z. exp. angew. Psychol.*, 1954, II, 92–135.

Mierke, K. *Wille und Leistung.* Göttingen: Hogrefe, 1955.

Miles, G. H. Achievement drive and habitual modes of task approach as factors in skill transfer. *J. exp. Psychol.*, 1958, 55, 156–162.

Milholland, J. E. Note on the further validation of the Alpert-Haber Achievement Anxiety Test. *J. abnorm. soc. Psychol.*, 1964, 69, 236.

Miller, D. R., & Swanson, G. E. The study of conflict. In M. R. Jones (Ed.), *Nebraska symposium on motivation 1956.* Lincoln, Neb.: Univer. of Nebraska Press, 1956, Pp. 137–173.

Miller, D. R., & Swanson, G. E. *The changing American parent.* New York: Wiley, 1958.

Miller, K. S., & Worchel, P. The effects of need-achievement and self-ideal discrepancy of performance under stress. *J. Pers.*, 1956, 25, 176–190.

Miller, N. E. Experimental studies of conflict. In J. McV. Hunt (Ed.), *Personality and the behavior disorders.* Vol. I. New York: Ronald, 1944. Pp. 431–465.

Miller, N. E. Liberalization of basic S-R concepts: Extension of conflict behavior, motivation, and social learning. In S. Koch (Ed.), *Psychology: A study of a science*. Vol. 2. New York: McGraw-Hill, 1959. Pp. 196–292.

Minor, C. A., & Neel, R. G. The relationship between achievement motive and occupational preference. *J. counsel. Psychol.*, 1958, 5, 39–43.

Mischel, W. Delay of gratification, need for achievement, and acquiescence in another culture. *J. abnorm. soc. Psychol.*, 1961, 62, 543–552.

Mitchell, J. V. An analysis of the factorial dimensions of the achievement motivation construct. *J. educ. Psychol.*, 1961, 52, 179–187.

Mittag, H.-D. Über personale Bedingungen des Gedächtnisses für Handlungen. Z. *Psychol.*, 1955, 158, 40–120.

Morgan, II. H. A psychometric comparison of achieving and non-achieving college students of high ability. *J. consult. Psychol.*, 1952, 16, 292–298.

Morgan, J. N. The achievement motive and economic behavior. *Econ. Develpm. cult. Change*, 1964, 12, 243–267.

Morrow, W. R., & Wilson, R. C. Family relations of bright high-achieving and under-achieving high school boys. *Child Develpm.*, 1961, 32, 501–510.

Moss, H. A., & Kagan, J. Stability of achievement and recognition seeking behaviors from early childhood through adulthood. *J. abnorm. soc. Psychol.*, 1961, 62, 504–513.

Moulton, R. W. Notes for a projective measure for fear of failure. 1958. In J. W. Atkinson, 1958c. Pp. 563–571.

Moulton, R. W. Effects of success and failure on level of aspiration as related to achievement motives. *J. Pers. soc. Psychol.*, 1965, 1, 399–406.

Moulton, R. W., Raphelson, A. C., Kristofferson, A. B., & Atkinson, J. W. The achievement motive and perceptual sensitivity under two conditions of motive arousal. 1958. In J. W. Atkinson, 1958c. Pp. 350–359.

Mowrer, O. H. *Learning theory and behavior*. New York: Wiley, 1960.

Mücher, H., & Heckhausen, H. Influence of mental activity and achievement motivation on skeletal muscle tonus. *Percept. mot. Skills*, 1962, 14, 217–218.

Müller, Anne. Über die Entwicklung des Leistungs-Anspruchsniveaus. Z. *Psychol.*, 1958, 162, 238–253.

Murray, H. A. *Explorations in personality*. New York: Oxford Univer. Press, 1938.

Murray, H. A. *Thematic Apperception Test manual*. Cambridge, Mass.: Harvard Univer. Press, 1943.

Murray, H. A. Toward a classification of interactions. In T. Parsons & E. A. Shils (Eds.), *Toward a general theory of action*. Cambridge, Mass.: Harvard Univer. Press, 1951. Pp. 434–464.

Murstein, B. I. The relationship of expectancy of reward to achievement performance on an arithmetic and thematic test. *J. consult. Psychol.*, 1963, **27**, 394–399.

Murstein, B. I., & Collier, H. L. The role of the TAT in the measurement of achievement as a function of expectancy. *J. proj. Tech.*, 1962, **26**, 96–101.

Nicholson, W. M. The influence of anxiety upon learning: interference or drive increment? *J. Pers.*, 1958, **26**, 303–319.

Nuttall, R. L. Some correlates of high need for achievement among urban northern Negroes. *J. abnorm. soc. Psychol.*, 1964, **68**, 593–600.

Nuttin, J. *Tâche, réussite et échec*. Louvain: Univer. de Louvain Press, 1953.

Ovsiankina, Maria. Die Wiederaufnahme unterbrochener Handlungen. *Psychol. Forsch.*, 1928, **11**, 302–379.

Peak, Helen. The effect of arousal motivation on attitudes. *J. abnorm. soc. Psychol.*, 1960, **61**, 463–468.

Piaget, J. *La naissance de l'intelligence chez l'enfant*. Neuchâtel Paris: Delachaux & Niestlé, 1936.

Poffenberger, T., & Norton, D. Sex differences in achievement motive in mathematics as related to cultural change. *J. genet. Psychol.*, 1963, **103**, 341–350.

Pottharst, Barbara C. The achievement motive and level of aspiration after experimentally induced success and failure. Unpublished doctoral dissertation, Univer. of Michigan, 1955 (cf. Atkinson, 1958c, p. 299).

Raphelson, A. C. The relationships among imaginative, direct verbal, and physiological measures of anxiety in an achievement situation. *J. abnorm. soc. Psychol.*, 1957, **54**, 13–18.

Raphelson, A. C., & Moulton, R. W. The relationship between imaginative and direct verbal measures of test anxiety under two conditions of uncertainty. *J. Pers.*, 1958, **26**, 556–567.

Ray, W. S. Mild stress and problem solving. *Amer. J. Psychol.*, 1965, **78**, 227–234.

Raynor, J. O., & Smith, C. P. Achievement-related motives and risk taking in games of skill and chance. Princeton Univer., 1965 (mimeographed paper).

Reimanis, G. Disparity theory and achievement motivation. *J. abnorm. soc. Psychol.*, 1964, **69**, 206–210.

Reissman, L. Levels of aspiration and social class. *Amer. sociol. Rev.*, 1953, **18**, 233–242.

Reiter, H. H. Some personality correlates of the Page Fantasy Scale. *Percept. mot. Skills*, 1963, **16**, 747–748.

Reitman, E. E., & Williams, C. D. Relationships between hope of success and fear of failure, anxiety, and need for achievement. *J. abnorm. soc. Psychol.*, 1961, **62**, 465–467.

Reitman, W. R. Motivational induction and the behavior correlates of the achievement and affiliation motives. *J. abnorm. soc. Psychol.*, 1960, **60**, 8–13.

Reitman, W. R. Need achievement, fear of failure, and selective recall. *J. abnorm. soc. Psychol.*, 1961, **62**, 142–144.

Reitman, W. R., & Atkinson, J. W. Some methodological problems in the use of thematic apperceptive measures of human motives. 1958. In J. W. Atkinson, 1958c. Pp. 664–683.

Ricciuti, H. N., & Sadacca, R. The prediction of academic grades with a projective test of achievement motivation: II. Cross-validation at the high school level. Princeton, N.J.: *Res. Bull. Educ. Testing Service*, 1955.

Ricciuti, H. N., & Schultz, D. G. Level of aspiration measures and self-estimates of personality in relation to achievement motivation. Princeton, N.J.: *Res. Bull. Educ. Testing Service*, 1954.

Rim, Y. Risk-taking and need for achievement. *Acta Psychol.*, 1963, **21**, 108–115.

Robinowitz, R. Attributes of pupils achieving beyond their level of expectancy. *J. Pers.*, 1956, **24**, 308–317.

Robinson, W. P. The measurement of achievement motivation. Doctoral thesis, Univer. of Oxford, 1961.

Robinson, W. P. An experiment to investigate the relationship between a level of aspiration and *n* achievement in academically successful and unsuccessful boys. Unpublished manuscript, Univer. of Hull, 1962. (a)

Robinson, W. P. Atkinson's theory of risk-taking behavior. A theoretical and empirical evaluation. Unpublished manuscript, Univer. of Hull, 1962. (b)

Robinson, W. P. The achievement motive, academic success, and intelligence test score. *Brit. J. soc. clin. Psychol.*, 1964, **4**, 98–103.

Rosen, B. C. The achievement syndrome. *Amer. sociol. Rev.*, 1956, **21**, 203–211. (Also in Atkinson, 1958c).

Rosen, B. C. Race, ethnicity, and the achievement syndrome. *Amer. sociol. Rev.*, 1959, **24**, 47–60.

Rosen, B. C. Family structure and achievement motivation. *Amer. sociol. Rev.*, 1961, **26**, 574–585.

Rosen, B. C. Socialization and the achievement motivation in Brazil. *Amer. sociol. Rev.*, 1962, **27**, 612–624.

Rosen, B. C., & D'Andrade, R. The psychosocial origins of achievement motivation. *Sociometry*, 1959, **22**, 185–218.

Rosenfeld, H. M. Social choice conceived as a level of aspiration. *J. abnorm. soc. Psychol.*, 1964, **68**, 491–500.

Rosenzweig, S. Preferences in the repetition of successful and unsuccessful activities as a function of age and personality. *J. genet. Psychol.*, 1933, **42**, 423–441.

Rosenzweig, S. Experimental study of repression with specific reference to need-persistive and ego-defensive reactions to frustration. *J. exp. Psychol.*, 1943, **32**, 64–74.

Rosenzweig, S. Further comparative data on repetition-choice after success and failure as related to frustration tolerance. *J. genet. Psychol.*, 1945, **66**, 75–81.

Rotter, J. B. *Social learning and clinical psychology.* New York: Prentice-Hall, 1954.

Ryan, D. E., & Lakie, W. L. Competitive and noncompetitive performance in relation to achievement motive and manifest anxiety. *J. Pers. soc. Psychol.*, 1965, **1**, 342–345.

Samelson, F. The relation of achievement and affiliation motives to conforming behavior in two conditions of conflict with a majority. In J. W. Atkinson (Ed.), *Motives in fantasy, action, and society.* Princeton, N.J.: Van Nostrand, 1958. Pp. 421–433.

Sampson, E. E. Birth order, need achievement, and conformity. *J. abnorm. soc. Psychol.*, 1962, **64**, 155–159.

Sampson, E. E. Achievement in conflict. *J. Pers.*, 1963, **31**, 510–516.

Sarason, I. G. The effects of anxiety and threat on the solution of a difficult task. *J. abnorm. soc. Psychol.*, 1961, **62**, 165–168.

Sarason, S. B., Mandler, G., & Craighill, P. C. The effect of differential instructions on anxiety and learning. *J. abnorm. soc. Psychol.*, 1952, **47**, 561–565.

Schlosberg, H. Three dimensions of emotion. *Psychol. Rev.*, 1954, **61**, 81–88.

Schmidt, H. D., & Zarn, R. Erfolg und Misserfolg als Determinanten einiger Entscheidungsparameter. Z. Psychol., 1964, 169, 18–34.

Schönpflug, W. Über Aktivationsprozesse im Lernversuch. Psychol. Arbeiten, 1963, 8. Frankfurt a.M.: Kramer.

Schubert-Jäckel, Gerda, & Mehl, J. Über die Erfassung der Leistungsmotivation mit Bildmaterial. Z. Psychol., 1962, 166, 182–224.

Scodel, A., Ratoosh, P. & Minas, J. S. Some personality correlates of decision making under conditions of risk. Behavioral Sci., 1959, 4, 19–28.

Scott, W. A. The avoidance of threatening material in imaginative behavior. J. abnorm. soc. Psychol., 1956, 52, 338–346. (Also in J. W. Atkinson, 1958c).

Sears, Pauline S. Levels of aspiration in academically successful and unsuccessful children. J. abnorm. soc. Psychol., 1940, 35, 498–536.

Sears, Pauline S., & Levin, H. Level of aspiration in preschool children. Child Develpm., 1957, 28, 317–326.

Shaw, M. C. Need achievement scales as predictors of academic success. J. educ. Psychol., 1961, 52, 282–285.

Shaw, M. C., & Dutton, B. E. The use of the parent attitude research inventory with the parents of bright academic underachievers. J. educ. Psychol., 1962, 53, 203–208.

Shipley, T. E., & Veroff, J. A projective measure of need for affiliation. J. exp. Psychol., 1952, 43, 349–356.

Silverman, J. Self-esteem and differential responsiveness to success and failure. J. abnorm. soc. Psychol., 1964, 69, 115–118.

Singer, J. L., & Rowe, R. An experimental study of some relationships between daydreaming and anxiety. J. consult. Psychol., 1962, 26, 446–454.

Singer, J. L., & Schonbar, Rosalea A. Correlates of daydreaming: a dimension of self awareness. J. consult. Psychol., 1961, 25, 1–6.

Sliosberg, Sarah. Zur Dynamik des Ersatzes in Spiel- und Ernstsituationen. Psychol. Forsch., 1934, 19, 122–181.

Slotnik, R. S., Liebert, R. M. & Hilgard, E. R. The enhancement of muscular performance in hypnosis through exhortation and involving instructions. J. Pers., 1965, 33, 37–45.

Slovic, P. Convergent validation of risk-taking measures. J. abnorm. soc. Psychol., 1962, 65, 68–71.

Smith, C. P. Achievement-related motives and goal setting under different conditions. J. Pers., 1963, 31, 124–140.

Smith, C. P. Relationships between achievement-related motives and intelligence, performance level, and persistence. *J. abnorm. soc. Psychol.*, 1964, **68**, 523–533.

Smock, C. D. Recall of interrupted and non-interrupted tasks as a function of experimentally induced anxiety and motivational relevance of the task stimuli. *J. Pers.*, 1957, **25**, 589–599.

Spence, K. W. A theory of emotionally based drive (D) and its relation to performance in simple learning situations. *Amer. Psychol.*, 1958, **13**, 131–141.

Spitzer, Ilse. Untersuchungen über die Einflüsse der erhöhten Motivation auf Konzentrations- und Intelligenzleistungen. *Psychol. Beitr.*, 1961, **V**, 559–576.

Stanford, Diane, Dember, W. N., & Stanford, L. B. A children's form of the Alpert-Haber Achievement Anxiety Scale. *Child Develpm.*, 1963, **34**, 1027–1032.

Stauder, K. H. Über den Pensionierungsbankrott. *Psyche*, 1955, **IX**, 481–497.

Steiner, I. O. Self-perception and goal-setting behavior. *J. Pers.*, 1957, **25**, 344–355.

Stennet, R. G. The relationship of performance level to level of arousal. *J. exp. Psychol.*, 1957, **54**, 54–61.

Strauss, M. A. Deferred gratification, social class and the achievement syndrome. *Amer. sociol. Rev.*, 1962, **27**, 326–335.

Strodtbeck, F. L. Family interaction, values, and achievement. In D. C. McClelland *et al.* (Eds.), *Talent and society*. Princeton, N.J.: Van Nostrand, 1958. Pp. 135–194.

Suedfeld, P., Grissom, R. J., & Vernon, J. The effects of sensory deprivation and social isolation on the performance of an unstructured cognitive task. *Amer. J. Psychol.*, 1964, **77**, 111–115.

Surwillo, W. W. Psychological factors in muscle-action potentials: EMG gradients. *J. exp. Psychol.*, 1956, **52**, 263–272.

Taylor, Janet A. A personality scale of manifest anxiety. *J. abnorm. soc. Psychol.*, 1953, **48**, 285–290.

Taylor, Janet A. Drive theory and manifest anxiety. *Psychol. Bull.*, 1956, **53**, 303–320.

Taylor, Janet A., & Spence, K. W. The relationship of anxiety level to performance in serial learning. *J. exp. Psychol.*, 1952, 44, 61–64.

Teahan, J. E. Future time perspective, optimism, and academic achievement. *J. abnorm. soc. Psychol.*, 1958, **57**, 379–380.

Tent, L. Untersuchungen zur Erfassung des Verhältnisses von

Anspannung und Leistung bei vorwiegend psychisch bean-spruchenden Tätigkeiten. *Arch. ges. Psychol.*, 1963, **115**, 105–172.

Thomae, H. Einfluss des Elternhauses auf das Verhältnis der Jugendlichen zur Leistung. *Psychol.u.Praxis*, 1956, **1**, 22–32.

Thomas, F. H. Visualization, experience, and motivation as related to feedback in problem solving. *Amer. Psychologist*, 1956, **11**, 444.

Uhlinger, Carolyn A., & Stephens, M. W. Relation of achievement motivation to academic achievement in students of superior ability. *J. educ. Psychol.*, 1960, **51**, 259–266.

Veroff, J. Theoretical background for studying the origins of human motivational dispositions. *Merrill-Palmer Quart. Behav. Develpm.*, 1965, **11**, 3–18.

Veroff, J., Wilcox, Sue, & Atkinson, J. W. The achievement motive in high school and college age women. *J. abnorm. soc. Psychol.*, 1953, **48**, 108–119.

Veroff, J., Atkinson, J. W., Feld, Sheila, C., & Gurin, G. The use of thematic apperception to assess motivation in a nationwide interview study. *Psychol. Monogr.*, 1960, **74**, No. 12 (Whole No. 499)

Veroff, J., Feld, Sheila C., & Gurin, G. Achievement motivation and religious background. *Amer. sociol. Rev.*, 1962, **27**, 205–217.

Veroff, J., Feld, Sheila C., & Crockett, H. J. Explorations into the effects of picture cues on thematic apperceptive expression of achievement motivation. *J. Pers. soc. Psychol.*, 1966, **3**, 171–181.

Vogel, W., Baker, R. W., & Lazarus, R. S. The role of motivation in psychological stress. *J. abnorm. soc. Psychol.*, 1958, **56**, 105–112.

Vogel, W., Raymond, Susan, & Lazarus, R. S. Intrinsic motivation and psychological stress. *J. abnorm. soc. Psychol.*, 1959, **58**, 225–233.

Vukovich, A., Heckhausen, H., & von Hatzfeld, Annette. Konstruktion eines Fragebogens zur Leistungsmotivation. Unpublished manuscript, Univer. of Münster, 1964.

Wagner, R. F., & Williams, J. F. An analysis of speech behavior in groups differing in achievement imagery and defensiveness. *J. Pers.*, 1961, **29**, 1–9.

Walker, E. L., & Heyns, R. W. *An anatomy for conformity*. Englewood Cliffs, N.J.: Prentice Hall, 1962.

Wapner, S., Werner, H., & Krus, D. M. The effect of success and failure on space localization. *J. Pers.*, 1957, **25**, 752–756.

Weber, M. Die protestantische Ethik und der Geist des Kapitalismus. *Arch. Sozialwiss. u. Sozialpolitik*, 1904, **20**, 1–54; 1905, **21**, 1–110.

Weiner, B. Need Achievement and the resumption of incompleted tasks. *J. Pers. soc. Psychol.*, 1965, **1**, 165–168. (a)

Weiner, B. The effects of unsatisfied achievement motivation on persistence and subsequent performance. *J. Pers.*, 1965, **33**, 428–442. (b)

Weiner, B. The role of success and failure in the learning of easy and complex tasks. *J. Pers. soc. Psychol.*, 1966, **3**, 339–344.

Weiner, B., & Rosenbaum, R. M. Determinants of choice between achievement- and nonachievement-related activities. *J. exp. Res. Pers.*, 1965, **1**, 114–121.

Weiss, P., Wertheimer, M., & Groesbeck, B. Achievement motivation, academic aptitude, and college grades. *Educ. psychol. Measmt.*, 1959, **19**, 663–666.

Wendt, H. W. Motivation, effort, and performance. In D. C. McClelland (Ed.), *Studies in motivation*. New York: Appleton, 1955. Pp. 448–459.

Wendt, H. W. Risk-taking as a function of pre-verbal "imprinting"? Some data and speculations. *Arch. ges. Psychol.*, 1961, **113**, 325–350.

Wendt, H. W. Points of origin for infant ecologies: religion and purchase of devices affecting pre-verbal mobility. *Psychol. Rep.*, 1965, **16**, 209–210.

Wertheim, J., & Mednick, S. A. The achievement motive and field independence. *J. consult. Psychol.*, 1958, **22**, 38.

Wertheimer, M. *Produktives Denken*. Frankfurt a.M.: Kramer, 1957.

White, R. W. Motivation reconsidered: The concept of competence. *Psychol. Rev.*, 1959, **66**, 297–333.

White, R. W. Competence and the psychosexual stages of development. In M. R. Jones (Ed.), *Nebraska Symposium on motivation 1960*. Lincoln, Neb.: Univer. Nebraska Press, 1960. Pp. 97–141.

Williams, J. E. Mode of failure, interference tendencies, and achievement imagery. *J. abnorm. soc. Psychol.*, 1955, **51**, 573–580.

Winterbottom, Marian R. The relation of need for achievement to learning experiences in independence and mastery. 1958. In J. W. Atkinson, 1958c. Pp. 453–478.

Wolf, Theta H. The effect of praise and competition on the persisting behavior of kindergarten children. *Inst. Child Welfare Monogr. Series*, 1938, **15**, 1–138. Univer. of Minnesota Press.

Wolff, W. *Expression of personality*. New York: Harper, 1943.

Woodworth, R. S. *Dynamics of behavior*. New York: Holt, 1958.

Yerkes, R. M., & Dodson, J. D. The relation of strength of stimulus to rapidity of habit formation. *J. comp. neurol. Psychol.*, 1908, **18**, 459–482.

Young, P. T. The role of affective processes in learning and motivation. *Psychol. Rev.*, 1959, **66**, 104–125.

Zazzo, Bianka. La représentation de la réussite chez les adolescents. *Psychol. Franç.*, 1963, **VIII**, 138–139.

Zeigarnik, Bluma. Über das Behalten von erledigten und unerledigten Handlungen. *Psychol. Forsch.*, 1927, **9**, 1–85.

Zelen, S. L. Behavioral criteria and Rorschach measures of level of aspiration and rigidity. *J. Pers.*, 1954, **23**, 207–214.

Zunich, M. Children's reaction to failure. *J. genet. Psychol.*, 1964, **104**, 19–24.

AUTHOR INDEX

Numbers in italics indicate the pages on which complete references are given.

195

198 AUTHOR INDEX

Katchmar, L. T., 107, *178*
Katkovsky, W., 148, 153, 155, 156, *170, 178*
Katona, G., 134, *179*
Katz, D., 58, *179*
Katz, F. M., 22, 23, 29, 77, *179*
Kausler, D. H., 74, 100, *179*
Keister, M. E., 150, *179*
Kellaway, R., 52, *170*
Kemmler, L., 11, 13, 17, 50, 57, 70, 129, 132, 136, 142, 151, 154, *176, 184*
Kiekheben-Roelofsen, I., 62, 118, 143, 144, *176*
Kimble, G. A., 115, *178*
Kimbrough, W. W., 20, *177*
Kissel, S., 108, *178*
Klamma, M., 142, *179*
Klauer, K. J., 137, 138, *179*
Klineberg, O., 33, 94, *180*
Knapp, R. H., 15, 22, 29, 44, 45, 80, 161, *175, 179, 183*
Kohn, M. L., 29, *179*
Kolb, D. A., 161, *179*
Kornadt, H.-J., 10, *180*
Krauss, R. M., 78, 119, 120, *175*
Krawitz, R. N., 18, 19, *180*
Krebs, A. M., 65, 155, *180*
Kristofferson, A. B., 72, 76, 136, 137, *185*
Krugman, A. D., 161, *180*
Krumboltz, J. D., 19, 128, *180*
Krus, D. M., 118, *191*
Künkel, F., 24, 43, *180*

L

Lakie, W. L., 56, 76, 135, *188*
Lambert, W. E., 33, 94, *180*
Lazarus, R. S., 13, 49, 70, 73, 75, 106, 107, 108, 109, 110, 135, 136, 138, 140, *180, 191*
Leader, F. B., 143, *183*
Lersch, P., 35, *180*
Leshan, L. L., 29, 41, *180*

Lesser, G. S., 13, 18, 19, 30, 73, 134, *174, 180*
Leuba, C., 143, *180*
Levin, H., 146, 148, *180, 189*
Lewin, K., 1, 41, 44, 46, 53, 84, 90, 109, 141, 145, *180, 181*
Lewis, H. B., 46, 119, *181*
Liberman, A. M., 16, 75, 137, *183*
Liberty, P., 23, 94, *168*
Liebert, R. M., 105, 106, *189*
Lindsley, D. B., 106, *181*
Littig, L. W., 30, 31, 60, 79, 94, 95, 108, 131, *179, 181*
Litwin, G. H., 15, 32, 60, 74, 78, 79, 93, 94, 95, 98, 100, 101, 102, 114, 132, 133, *166, 181, 184*
Lowell, E. L., 2, 4, 12, 14, 17 18, 42, 65, 70, 128, 130, 132, 133, 134, 136, 137, 139, 151, 158, *181, 183*
Luchins, A. R., 134, *181*

Mc

McArthur, C. C., 16, *182*
McCall, R. J., 141, *182*
McClelland, D. C., 2, 4, 6, 7, 8, 9, 12, 14, 15, 16, 17, 18, 19, 20, 23, 28, 29, 31, 32, 33, 34, 42, 43, 44, 60, 61, 62, 65, 70, 75, 80, 91, 93, 94, 95, 99, 102, 115, 128, 129, 130, 132, 133, 134, 135, 136, 137, 138, 139, 145, 151, 152, 153, 156, 158, 159, 160, 161, 162, *169, 170, 178, 182, 183*
McKeachie, W. J., 30, 32, 74, 109, 110, 132, 139, 160, *169, 183*
McKee, J., 143, *183*

M

Maddox, H., 114, *183*
Mahler, W., 36, 46, 47, 63, *183*
Mahone, C. H., 93, 128, *183*
Malmo, R. B., 106, *183*
Mandler, G., 16, 107, 108, *183, 188*
Marlowe, D., 8, 132, *183*
Marrow, A. J., 121, *184*

SUBJECT INDEX

A

Ability, native, 127, 129–131, 140
Accomplishments, 127–140
  intelligence tests, 128
  scholastic achievement, 131–133
  tasks, 133–140
Achievement Anxiety Test (AAT),
  8, 16, 110, 132–133
Achievement in school and college,
  131–133
  improvement of, 162
  in psychology courses, 132
  prediction based on intelligence
    and anxiety measures, 132–133
  teaching style and, 110–111
Achievement motivation, 2, 4–6
  as instrumental motive system, 35
  conflict with other motives, 64–66
  definition of, 4–5
  experience, dimensions of, 39–52
  goal and performance structure of,
    67–68
  indices of, 7–9, 14–17, 98–99, 102,
    107, 123
  in females, 17–19
  origin of, 141–146, 148–150
  prediction of, long range, 20, 146–
    147
  raising of in adults, 162
  situational structure of, basic, 143
  social learning, as product of, 148–
    162

  theme of, 4–6, 24–29, 39–41, 48,
    69–71, 73, 108
  unreal normative states in, 48
Achievement Motivation measure
  (AM), 16–17, 23, 43–44, 50, 57,
  75, 101, 111, 129, 134, *see also*
  Fear of failure, Hope of success
  activation and, 107–108
  children, testing method for, 17
  measurement, 16–17
  need Achievement, correlation
    with, 16–17
  reliability
    scoring, 19
    test-retest, 20
  success vs. failure-motivated per-
    sons, 22–24
  validation, 17
  wish fulfillment in fantasies and,
    48
Achievement tasks, 133–140
  coding, 115–116, 135–136
  cognitive styles, tests of, 136
  conceptual problems, 111, 113–
    114, 134
  mental arithmetic problems, 137–
    139
  perceptual learning, 135
  sensorimotor tasks, 101, 106, 108,
    115–116, 135
  speed tests, simple, 135–136, 138–
    139

success vs. failure-oriented, 21–23, 27, 40–41

transferability of, 25

transmitted by parents, 153–154, 157–158, 160

unreal ones, 48

value systems, embedded in, 34–37

Examination, 57–58, 96, 113–114, 121–122

Expectation, *see also* Success probabilities

in small children, 145

of failure, 23, 53–58, 110

of parents, 153

of success, 22–23, 145, 148

Expectation gradient, *see* *also* Motive arousal

as feedback result, 109, 125

determinants of, 3, 70–72, 77–78, 80

energy output and, 105–106

in time perspective, 42–43

thematic apperceptive production and, 10–11

Experimenter effect, 74, 112

Expressive behavior, *see also* Doodle measure

after success and failure, 62, 118, 151

in handwriting, 107

F

Failure

ability to differentiate between chance and skill factors, 60

characteristics of, 5–6, 85–86

coping with in early childhood, 61–64, 144, 146–147, 150–151

evaluative disposition, future-oriented, 21–23, 41, 108

expectation of, 23, 100

expressive behavior after, 62, 118, 150–151

feedback about, 109–113

in early childhood, experience of, 50, 143–145

reactions to, 61–64, 151–152

self-deceptions, 48, 62

social contact after, 62, 148

self-esteem in 2- to 3-year olds and, 40

social vs. self-oriented dimension, 23

Failure motivation, *see* Fear of failure

Family structure

broken homes, 159

completeness of family, 30–31

size of family, 158

Fantasy

satiation effects, 19–20

substitute function of, 47–49

wish fulfillment in and achievement motivation, 48

Fear of failure

accomplishments and, 129–130, 132–136, 138–139

arousal effects, paradoxial, 13, 57

criterion variables of, 16

daydreaming, increased by, 49

development of, 64, 147–148

difficulty of task and, ratings of, 57–58

facilitating vs. debilitating anxiety, 110

failure-motivated person, 22–24, 109

in children, 61–64, 146–147

level of aspiration and, 50, 54, 92–103

measurement of, 16–17, 98–99, 102, 110, 123

persistence and, 55–56, 113–114

reliability, scoring, 19

reliability, test-retest, 20

retrospective judgment of success and, 125

risk-taking and, 59

I

Identification
    learning, 153, 162
    with father as model, 158
    with parents, 154
Incentive value
    attainability of goal and, 78–80,
        120
    cultural values, 35
    free time, gaining additional, 73,
        113
    games of chance, 60–61, 72, 79
    goals distant in time, 80–81
    intelligence test for success- and
        failure-motivated persons, 57–58
    material or monetary rewards, 29,
        32, 35, 60, 72, 75–77, 95, 160
    of different occupations as index of
        achievement motivation, 15
    paced vs. nonpaced work, 111,
        138–139
    substitute activities, 47, 62–63, 81
    success probabilities, 5, 50–51, 53–
        56, 74–75, 78, 99
    teaching styles, 110–111, 139
    trivial tasks, 75, 138–139
Independence, *see also* Child-
        rearing practices
    as result of religious trends, 33
    critical period of training in, 154–
        156
    in routine skills, 142, 152
    in sensorimotor vs. conceptual
        activities, 142
    training of, 151–157, 160
India, 133, 158, 162
Individual psychology, 24
Indulgence, 153, 155
Inertial tendencies, 100
Inhibition
    proactive, 116
    reactive, 115–116
    retroactive, 116
Inhibitory tendencies, *see* Avoidance
        behavior
Intelligence and achievement moti-
        vation, 128–131
    complementary relationship of,
        128–129
    in child development, 130
    in homogeneous socioeconomic
        groups, 130–131
    interaction of, 130–133, 147
    in samples of higher intelligence,
        129–131
Iowa Picture Interpretation Test
    (IPIT), 15, 116, 134–135

J

Japan
    child-rearing practices, 152, 154,
        158
    female subjects, 18
Jews, 31–32, 161
Judgment of success in retrospec-
        tion, 124–125

L

Learning theory, 112–113, 148–151,
    157–158, *see also* Reinforcement
Leisure time, 114, 118
Level of aspiration, 84–103
    Atkinson's risk-taking model, 97,
        99–101
    behavior, inferred from, 84
    conflict in, 54–55, 89–92
    conflict between standards of ex-
        cellence, 89–90
    definitions, 83–86
    distance away in time, 90
    evaluative disposition, character-
        istic of, 24, 86–87
    goal discrepancy, 85, 87, 91
    goal setting, contrasted with, 84
    importance of task, 89
    in career goals, 93–94
    in feebleminded children, 149–150
    individual differences in, 86–87,
        89–92

reality and, degree of, 46–47
social class and, 41
Training program
  achievement motivation, raising of,
    161–162
  failure reactions, changing of, 151
  in mechanical skills, 133
Turkey, 159

U

Uncertainty, *see* Success probabilities
Underachievement vs. overachievement, 136, 161
  child-rearing practices and, 151–
    152, 156
  need Achievement scores to differ-
    ent picture cues and, 18–19
United States
  achievement motivation and re-
    ligious background, 161
  broken homes, effect of, 159
  child-rearing practices, 151–160
  female subjects, 17–19
  Germany, compared with, 29
  need Achievement in children's
    readers, 33
  social strata, 29

V

Valence, 69–81, *see also* Incentive
  value
  attractiveness of task, 75, 78, 99,
    120
  resultant valence theory, 99
  short-term change of, 78, 109, 120
  stability of achievement-related
    valence, 27–28
Validation of measures for achievement motivation
  by correlation with behavioral
    measures, 17

by planned variation in arousal
  conditions, 17–19, 70
Validity, *see* Validation
Value attitudes, *see* Evaluative disposition
Value orientation, *see* Evaluative disposition

W

Withdrawal, 55, 62–64, 94, 101–102,
  109, 111, 139
Work partner, choice of, 64–65, 79–
  80, 101

Z

Zeigarnik effect, 119–124
  achievement motivation and, 122–
    124
  by involuntary recall, 119
  correctness vs. completion of task,
    effect of, 121
  ego-defense in the disappearance
    of, 120, 122–123
  fear of failure arousal, indicative
    of, 76
  future time perspective and, 124
  important vs. unimportant tasks, of
    personally, 46
  in volunteering vs. nonvolunteer-
    ing subjects, 122
  lapse of time before recall, 122
  personality factors operative in,
    122–123
  self-oriented attitude, influenced
    by, 40
  success and failure stories, recall
    of, 123
  test conditions, depending on,
    119–123
  testing technique, problems of,
    119–122